THE
BASEBALL
BOOK
1987-88

THE BASEBALL BOOK 1987-88

ANDREW THOMAS

Macdonald
Queen Anne Press

In association with
Major League Baseball

A **Queen Anne Press** BOOK

© Andrew Thomas 1987

First published in Great Britain in 1987 by
Queen Anne Press, a division of
Macdonald & Co (Publishers) Ltd
3rd Floor
Greater London House
Hampstead Road
London NW1 7QX

A BPCC plc Company

Cover photographs – Front: Darryl Strawberry, New York Mets (*All-Sport*)
Back: Mets v. Red Sox in the World Series 1986 (*All-Sport*)
Dodgers Stadium, Los Angeles (*All-Sport*)

British Library Cataloguing in Publication Data
Thomas, Andrew
    The baseball book.
    1. Baseball
    I. Title
    796.357   GV867

    ISBN 0-356-15136-0

Typeset by Flair plan Photo-typesetting Limited
Printed and bound in Spain

PHOTOGRAPHS

All photographs have been supplied by courtesy of
Fotosports International, with the exception of All-Sport
22T, 42L, 58L, 97, 104, 117, 118, 119; Stephen Dunn 46L;
Los Angeles Dodgers 107; Mediawatch Ltd 32, 36, 42B,
53, 99T, 102, 106, 108, 113R; National Baseball Library
99L, 101; New York Yankees 70, 71R.

CONTENTS

INTRODUCTION

American professional Major League baseball has been played for more than 100 years, but for many people in Britain the televised highlights of the exciting 1985 World Series between Kansas City and St Louis, and the thrilling 1986 World Series between the New York Mets and the Boston Red Sox, were their first experiences of the game.

The encouraging audience ratings suggested that many on this side of the Atlantic had been as enthralled by the sight and sounds of America's premier sports series and the dramatic nature of all last year's post-season games as the 80,000,000 fans who watched them in the United States. Similar television coverage is planned in Britain throughout October this year and, as always, all the games will be broadcast live late into the night by the Armed Forces Radio and Television Service, which is relayed by AFN Europe radio.

Although baseball's rapidly increasing number of new fans and players in Britain could find out about the fundamentals of the game, its development and organisation from the introductory book, *A Guide to Baseball*, many also want to know more about amateur baseball here and overseas, its progress as an Olympic sport, but particularly, detailed information about the 26 Major League clubs, their players, all-time records, and aspects of organised baseball's history. All that is now available in this companion volume, *The Baseball Book 1987–88*. This new book should enable baseball fans of all ages, whether rookies new to the game, or old-timers, to become more closely involved in the rising tension and excitement of the 1987 Major League season, while identifying more fully with the sense of occasion and history which has helped the World Series become one of the world's great sports events.

Andrew Thomas, July 1987

Kevin McReynolds, New York Mets.

THE HISTORY AND DEVELOPMENT OF MAJOR LEAGUE BASEBALL

In 1845, New Yorker Alexander J. Cartwright led a committee which drafted standardised rules for the popular urban game of Town-ball, which had many of the essentials that we would recognise in modern baseball, not least, the use of a hard ball and the banning of 'plugging' the runner (i.e. being able to get him out by hitting him with the ball). The first game thought to have been played to Cartwright's rules was in 1846, when the New York Baseball Club beat the Knickerbockers 23–1 at St George's Cricket Club, Elysian Fields, Hoboken, New Jersey.

The game spread from the New York area to Philadelphia, and a measure of baseball's rapid acceptance was given in 1853 by the publication of the first baseball scorecard, or box-score in the *New York Clipper* newspaper.

In March 1858, a number of clubs in the New York City area became organised, with the formation of the National Association of Base Ball Players. This wholly amateur organisation amplified the Knickerbocker baseball rules and standardised measurements for both bat and ball. The organisation encouraged baseball in the smaller towns and villages of the area and on the Eastern college campuses.

The main competition to baseball at the time was from cricket, which was expanding, thanks to attractions such as the first All-England XI touring professionals, who played matches against the USA and Canada in 1859.

However, sporting rivalries were swept aside during the bitter years of the US Civil War. There are references in letters to suggest that soldiers on both sides played baseball and cricket, but the war not only brought about the defeat of the South, but also started to turn the tide against cricket's long-term development in America, outside its strongholds in the north-east.

After the Civil War, a hastily convened convention of ninety-one clubs met in New York in 1865 to reaffirm the standardised rules of baseball and in a forlorn attempt to preserve the game's wholly amateur status. Within only two years the National Association was alarmed to discover that the Rockford Baseball Club of Illinois and the Cincinnati Red Stockings of Ohio paid their players. The Cincinnati club, organised and managed by ex-cricketer Harry Wright, turned fully professional in 1869, paying between $600 and $1,400 for an eight-month tour. A further indication of the rising tide of professionalism was given when the Chicago White Stockings went to New Orleans for spring training. The inevitable break came in 1871 when the National Association of Professional Base Ball Players was formed in New York. Although this body was not a success, the writing was on the wall for the 'keep baseball amateur' lobby, and within a couple of seasons it had all but lost control of the game. Three years later, the professional Philadelphia Athletics and the Boston Red Stockings came to England and Ireland to play fourteen baseball games and seven cricket matches in a tour sponsored by Harry Wright.

In 1876, at the prompting of ex-cricketer A. G. Spalding, eight clubs, disillusioned with the National Association, not to mention the amount of drinking, gambling and corruption which had become associated with professional baseball, formed the National League, which exists to this day. In 1882, a second major league, the American Association was formed by eight clubs after a battle with the National League.

During the following stormy decade, the Union Association (1884) and Players' League (1890) and a number of minor leagues were formed. Many of the lesser clubs signed college boys who played for pay during their summer vacations, despite running the risk of losing their college eligibility.

In 1883 Moses Fleetwood Walker, a catcher for Toledo, of the American Association, became the first black to play for a major league club. He was soon followed by his brother and many others. Unfortunately, within four years a few whites, fearful that talented black players would swamp the major leagues, imposed a colour bar which lasted sixty years, and so deprived many great players from showing their skill in the majors. The banned men had to set up black leagues or play winter baseball in Latin American countries such as Mexico and Cuba.

In April 1947, Jackie Robinson broke the colour bar when he made his debut for the Brooklyn Dodgers of the National League. Although not the greatest black player of his day, he was considered the best equipped to handle the pressures of the situation. He went on to become the first black to play in the World Series, and won the National League's Most Valuable Player Award.

Following Robinson's dignified lead, other black players were signed by major league clubs and within twenty years they formed about 25 per cent of players. In 1975 Frank Robinson (no relation to Jackie) became the first black manager. However, by 1987, only 3 per cent of those in baseball's executive positions were from minority groups, and there is a concerted drive to increase this percentage. (The only black general manager,

Atlanta's Bill Lucas, died in 1979, aged only forty-three.)

In 1888–89, A. G. Spalding co-ordinated the first round-the-world baseball tour which successfully spread the American version of the game to New Zealand, Australia, Ceylon, Egypt, Italy, Ireland and Britain.

The newly formed English Baseball Association was reluctant to associate with the professional players, but All-Stars tours which included Britain took place in 1914 and 1924. The favoured destination in the 1930s, however, was Japan.

After barely a decade of competition, the American Association collapsed and merged with the National League to bring it to twelve teams. However, the new Western League, formed in 1893, was soon joined by four clubs from the National League, to form the American League which exists today. In 1901, after a two year 'war', the American League (eight teams) was recognised as a major league by the (eight club) National League. To cement the alliance, a three-man National Commission was set up to rule baseball, and in 1903 the inaugural World Series was played between the champion clubs of each league. Except for 1904 (when the New York Giants refused to play Boston) the World Series has been contested every October and become one of America's greatest sporting occasions.

By the turn of the century, professional baseball had become sufficiently part of America's expanding culture for poems such as 'Casey at the Bat' and 'Tinker, to Evers, to Chance', and baseball's enduring theme song 'Take me out to the Ball Game', to gain wide popularity.

Although cricket's chance of becoming a national game in America had already gone, it is ironic that the uneasy alliance between the two major leagues was made at the time when interest in cricket in America was at its height. In 1905, well over 350 matches were played around the game's American stronghold, Philadelphia, which also hosted the fifteenth touring team from England since 1859. On the 1908 tour to England, Philadelphia's John Barton King topped the English first-class bowling averages, and was generally reckoned to have been one of the finest cricketers in the world.

Between 1905–07, the bizarre proceedings of the Mills Commission (which was appointed at the prompting of baseball equipment manufacturer A. G. Spalding to determine the origin of baseball) brought uneasy parallels with claims made a decade or so earlier in England about the origins of rugby football. The committee's final report, in December 1907, stated that 'the first scheme for playing baseball, according to the best evidence obtainable to date, was devised by Abner Doubleday at Cooperstown, New York, in 1839'. This remakable statement raised little comment at the time, and as most of the documents collected were lost in a fire a decade later, it was not until the centenary of the 'event' that the claim was refuted by R. W. Henderson.

Just as Major League baseball was becoming well established, the professional game suffered a setback. In 1919, eight Chicago White Sox players were accused of deliberately losing the World Series to Cincinnati in what became known as the 'Black Sox Scandal'. Any evidence against the defendants was destroyed in a courthouse fire, with the result that all were found not guilty. However, the stern, conservative judge who presided in the case, K. M. Landis, banned the players involved soon after he was made the first Commissioner of Baseball (replacing the three-man National Commission) in 1920–21. Following the clear, moral stand taken by Commissioner Landis, the game's image recovered, and the game's folklore was soon enriched by many bitter-sweet moments.

The legendary home run hitter, George 'Babe' Ruth (who had made his name with Boston as a pitcher), was sold by the Boston Red Sox to the New York Yankees for $100,000 cash plus a $350,000 loan to the Boston owner. By 1930, Babe Ruth was paid $85,000 a year (a salary not matched for twenty-five years), and but for the insensitivity of such a rise during the Depression, he would have received more than $100,000.

Babe Ruth was the jewel in the Yankees' crown. He drew such large crowds that it was with some justification that Yankee Stadium became known as 'The House that Ruth Built'.

Ruth was to baseball what Don Bradman was to cricket. The two stars met at a Yankees v. White Sox game only months before the notorious 'body-line' Test Series of 1932–33. They can have had little in common except their genius with bat and ball. Stories about Ruth's real or imagined exploits, on and off the playing field, abound. After an American League All-Star tour to Japan near the end of his career, in 1934–35, Ruth returned home via Europe. In *The Babe Ruth Story* he tells how, when in London, he was taken to Lord's Cricket Ground, and hit the first ball bowled to him as far as anyone had seen, and then broke the bat in half on the second. Soon after he retired, Ruth was elected as one of the original inductees to baseball's Hall of Fame at Cooperstown.

In 1939 R. W. Henderson of the New York Public Library (which holds the Spalding Collection of baseball material), published a pamphlet entitled 'Ball, Bat and Bishop: The Origin of Ball Games', in which he refuted the 'Doubleday theory' proposed by the Mills Commission about thirty years before, and reaffirmed baseball's British roots.

Major League baseball continued to be played during the Second World War to help keep up morale, but night games were banned. After the attack on Pearl Harbor, the Chicago Cubs sent their redundant floodlights to the US Navy. The Cubs are now the only Major League team without lights, and cannot install any until a city ordinance is repealed.

About 60 per cent of Major League games are now played at night, and as more teams are likely to invest in roofed stadiums this percentage seems sure to increase.

Judge Landis died in office in 1944, and was succeeded as Commissioner by Senator A. B. Chandler. He resigned seven years later and was replaced by the ex-writer, broadcaster and National League President, Ford C. Frick.

In 1954 the glamour of Hollywood touched the game, when the star player of the New York Yankees, the 'Yankee Clipper' Joe DiMaggio, married film star Marilyn Monroe.

The ever-increasing popularity of Major League baseball and the rapid population increase in California during the 1950s prompted two blue-chip franchises, the New York Giants and the Brooklyn Dodgers, both steeped in tradition but going through difficult times in the East, to move to the West Coast.

Both leagues later expanded from eight to ten clubs, the American League in 1961 and the National League in 1962. In 1969 the number increased again, to twelve teams each. By this time Ford Frick, who had retired as Commissioner in 1965, had been succeeded for about three years by Air Force Lieutenant General William D. Eckert, before ex-National League attorney Bowie Kuhn successfully guided Organised Baseball through the upheavals of 1969. At this time, to increase the excitement for the fans, the leagues divided (largely on geographical grounds) into two divisions of East and West. The division winners playoff for the respective league pennants, with the two league champions meeting in the World Series.

In 1976, the American League expanded to fourteen clubs, and once three or four struggling franchises are on a more stable financial footing, the National League may follow suit.

The 1970s were years of increasing conflict between players and umpires and the management. Major League baseball's image of a carefree game played for fun changed to that of a big business corporation employing highly paid entertainers. There was a ten-day strike by players in 1971 and one lasting forty-five days by umpires eight years later. However, the most damaging players' strike, in every respect, lasted fifty-nine days and caused 714 games to be lost, in the split-season year of 1981.

In 1975–76 the old feudal Reserve Clause (or Reserve Rule) was severely modified and so opened the way to free agency and the wage explosion of the past decade financed by massive TV and radio contracts, and increasing advertising and attendance revenue. Hank Aaron became the first player to be paid over $200,000 in 1971. Eight years later Pete Rose and Nolan Ryan were paid $1,000,000. By 1986, the average salary was $400,000, and fifty-eight players were getting more than $1,000,000, topped by Gary Carter's $2,160,000.

After the inflated multi-year contracts of the last few years it would seem that an era of fiscal responsibility (called collusion by the suspicious players) may bring wages down over the next few seasons.

Bowie Kuhn resigned as Commissioner in 1984 and was succeeded by Peter V. Ueberroth, a self-made travel industry millionaire who had been thrust into the public eye as the organiser of the profitable 1984 Olympic Games in Los Angeles. As a parting gift, Kuhn made sure that Ueberroth was able to start his term as Commissioner with some of the office's original authority restored, following years of erosion by the club owners.

The American public may resent the intrusion of many of society's social ills at the ballpark, but Major League baseball has never been more popular. It would seem to have become more than just a game. Despite increasing radio and television (network, cable and satellite superstation) coverage, and increasing ticket prices, not to mention competition from a variety of leisure activities in an uncertain economic climate, attendances have doubled to over 47,500,000 in the past twenty years. Each of the twenty-six Major League teams attracted more than one million spectators to home games in 1986.

Baseball at all levels still attracts more spectators across America than horse racing, car racing, or American football, so may truly still be called America's national pastime.

Postal address: Major League Baseball
Headquarters,
350 Park Avenue,
New York,
NY 10022, USA.

Organised Baseball, or 'OB' as it is sometimes called, includes all the activities of the fourteen American League and twelve National League franchises of Major League baseball as well as the various minor leagues of professional baseball.

The following diary listing some of the events of the 1987 season gives an indication of the shape of the typical Major Leaguer's year, in which he may travel more than 45,000 miles.

1987

8 January:	Last day (until 1 May) for former clubs to resign players who are free agents.
1 February:	Salary arbitration hearings begin.
20 February:	The earliest date that pitchers, catchers and injured players may report for spring training.
25 February:	Full Major League squads report for spring training.
5 March:	Spring training schedule of about twenty games per club starts in Florida (Grapefruit League) and Arizona/California (Cactus League).
11 March:	Last date that contracts may be renewed for new season.
5 April:	Last day of spring training.
6 April:	Opening Day, the start of the Major League regular season of 162 games per club. The date by which each Major League club must reduce its forty-man winter rosters to a maximum of twenty-five players (a minimum of twenty-four active players).
1 May:	Former clubs may resign free agents who refuse contract arbitration in January. (Only five stars involved in 1987.)
2 June:	Start of summer free agent draft.
14 July:	58th annual All-Star game, at Oakland, California. The mid-season three-day break in the regular season.
27 July:	Annual Hall of Fame Game, at Cooperstown, New York.
1 September:	Major League club rosters may be expanded to forty players.
4 October:	Major League regular season ends.
6 October (approx):	Best of seven games, National League Championship Series starts, at East Division winner's stadium. Best of seven games, American League Championship Series starts, at West Division winner's ballpark.
17 October (approx):	1987 World Series starts, at the American League champion's ballpark. Best of seven games. A player has up to fifteen days after the 1987 World Series ends to file for free agency.
5–11 December:	Major League baseball's winter meetings.

GENERAL DIFFERENCES BETWEEN THE
TWO MAJOR LEAGUES

Unlike the professional American football teams of the NFL, clubs from the two rival Major League baseball leagues never meet in regular season play. Over the years, this isolation, slight rule differences, and the characteristics of particular ballparks have prompted the game to evolve a distinctive flavour in each league. While not all clubs in each league adhere slavishly to an AL or NL style of play, it is significant enough to be worth outlining here.

NATIONAL LEAGUE
Larger, modern stadiums,
9 out of the 12 are dual-use.
6 clubs play on grass, 6 on turf.
No designated hitter rule.
Pinch hitters used more often.
An average of 13 players per game.
The average game last 2 hrs 35 mins.
NL game based on speedy runners
and light hitters. A typical NL run
would be: a single, a stolen base,
and a sacrifice fly ball or bunt
to bring the run home.
In the World Series from 1970–86,
only 79 NL home runs,
but 72 stolen bases (of 111 attempts).
NL pitchers tend to throw fast, high
and inside pitches. This reduces the
chance of chop hits that bounce high
off artificial turf, and also gives the
catcher more time to throw out any
base runner attempting to steal.

About 280 NL batters are hit by
pitches in a season. (NL pitchers bat.)
The club that typifies the NL style
of play: St Louis Cardinals.

AMERICAN LEAGUE
Smaller, older ballparks,
only 6 out of 14 are dual-use.
10 clubs play on grass, 4 on turf.
A powerful designated hitter
used (see WS notes below).
An average of 11 players used per game.
25 per cent of games last over 3 hours.
AL game based on power hitters.
A typical AL run would be:
two batters walked on base by
the pitcher, then a home run to
clear the bases.
In the World Series from 1970–86,
87 AL home runs, but only
42 stolen bases (of 70 attempts).
AL pitchers tend to have more
Major League experience. They
throw more breaking pitches,
with a change of pace.
They try to keep pitches low in
the strike zone to encourage
more ground balls to be hit.
About 420 AL batters are hit by
pitches. (AL pitchers do not bat.)
The typical American League
ball club: California Angels.

THE NATIONAL LEAGUE

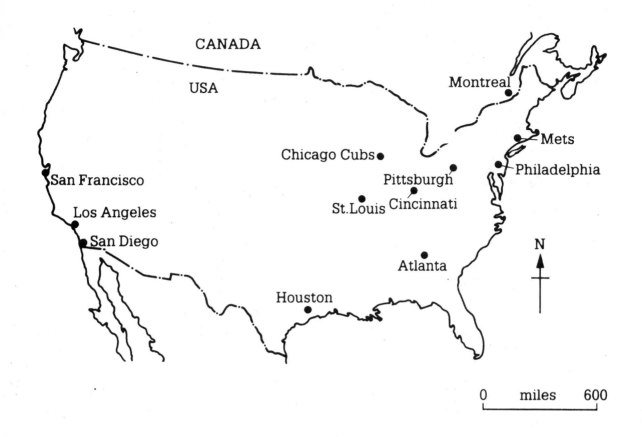

The National League was organised in 1876, twenty-four years before the rival American League, hence its somewhat misleading nickname, 'the senior circuit'.

Since the 1969 season, the National League has been divided into an East Division and West Division, which has six franchises in each.

West Division
Atlanta Braves
Cincinnati Reds
Houston Astros
Los Angeles Dodgers
San Diego Padres
San Francisco Giants

East Division
Chicago Cubs
Montreal Expos
New York Mets
Philadelphia Phillies
Pittsburgh Pirates
St Louis Cardinals

During the long regular season of 162 games per club, which lasts from early April until October, each team plays the other five clubs in its division eighteen times, nine games at home and nine away. Each one also plays the six teams in the other division twelve times, six games at home and six games away. The rivalries within each division are particularly strong in the National League, not only for historical reasons but also because it is vital for teams to do well against clubs in their own division. They play ninety games against those five, but just seventy-two games against the other six.

Of the 972 regular season games in 1987, 65 per cent were played at night and exactly 50 per cent on artificial turf.

At the end of the regular season the winners of each division playoff in the best of seven games NLCS (National League Championship Series) for the league pennant. The champion club then plays the American League champion in the annual World Series.

Club name: CHICAGO CUBS
League/Division: National, East
Postal address: Wrigley Field, 1060 West
Addison Street, Chicago,
Illinois 60613, USA
History of franchise: Chicago Cubs formed 1876
Won East Div. (since 1969): 1984
Won NL (since 1900): 1906, 07, 08, 10, 18, 29, 32, 35, 38, 45
Won World Series: 1907, 1908
Position in div. 1982 to 1986 5th, 5th, 1st, 4th, 5th
1987 spring training site: HoHokam Park, Mesa, Arizona
1987 Minor League farm club teams: AAA – Iowa; AA – Pittsfield; A – Winston-Salem, Peoria, Geneva; Rookie – Wytheville

Left: Pitcher Mike Mason, acquired from Texas (AL) during 1987.

Right: Wrigley Field, which may have floodlights for playoffs.

FACTS ABOUT WRIGLEY FIELD

Location: Addison Street, N. Clark St, Waveland
Ave & Sheffield Ave.
Capacity: 38,040
Playing surface: grass
1987 day games: 81 (+23 away)
    night games: none (+58 away) (no lights)
1987 ticket prices: $4 to $10.50
Radio: WGN 720 AM
TV and cable: WGN(9) Superstation

Ballpark details

For many fans Wrigley Field is the perfect ballpark
in which to watch Major League baseball. The
fans do not do 'The Wave' and there is a grass
field, ivy covered red-brick outfield walls, no flood-
light pylons, a hand operated scoreboard and the
flag hoisted after each game (blue with a white
'W' for a win, or white with a blue 'L' for a loss), all
factors which make it seem a treasured relic of a
bygone age.

One problem that sometimes affects games is
the strong wind from Lake Michigan which blasts
north-east Chicago from time to time and makes a
mockery of the game. The first NL game was
played in April 1916.

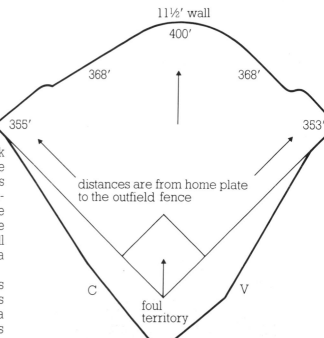

distances are from home plate
to the outfield fence

CHICAGO CUBS in 1987

Manager: Gene Michael, 2nd yr with Cubs, 4th yr in majors, W-136 L-131.

Cubs in '86: W-70 L-90 .438 finished 37 games behind NY Mets.

NL rankings: batting 3rd, pitching 12th.

Gene Michael views 1987 as a transition season for the club, particularly in view of the uncertain fitness of key pitchers. Besides improving basics, such as the team's indifferent outfielding (not helped by the long grass) and base running, more playing time is being given to the younger players such as Shawon Dunston (picked first in the 1982 draft, ahead of Dwight Gooden) and Greg Maddux. However, after an encouraging spring, and with long ball hitters such as Ryne Sandberg, Jody Davis, Lee Smith, Andre Dawson, plus fully recovered pitcher Rick Sutcliffe available, the Wrigley Field faithful may demand success now.

Pitching: Barring accidents, the rotation looks better with Rick Sutcliffe, Scott Sanderson, Mike Mason, Dickie Noles, Ed Lynch, rookie Greg Maddux, left-handers Steve Trout and Jamie Moyer. But star relief pitcher Lee Smith still has too little help from his bull pen colleagues.

Catcher: Jody Davis is one of the best, and has a good batter/catcher in Jim Sundberg, as his back-up.

Infielders: Leon Durham, All-Star second baseman Ryne Sandberg, and Shawon Dunston need support from Keith Moreland at the third base 'hot corner'.

Outfielders: Home run hitter free agent Andre Dawson (from the Expos), was just who Bob Dernier, Brian Dayett and Gary Matthews needed.

Leading reserves: Unsettled Jerry Mumphrey, Dave Martinez, and Manny Trillo.

Second baseman Ryne Sandberg – NL All-Star since 1984.

Club name: MONTREAL EXPOS
League/Division: National, East
Postal address: PO Box 500, Station M,
Montreal, Quebec, H1V 3P2,
Canada
History of franchise: Montreal Expos formed 1969
Won East Div. (since 1969): 1981
Yet to win NL or World Series
Position in div. 1982 to 1986: 3rd, 3rd, 5th, 3rd, 4th
1987 spring training site: Municipal Stadium, West Palm Beach, Florida (shared with Atlanta Braves)
1987 Minor League farm club teams: AAA – Indianapolis; AA – Jacksonville; A – West Palm Beach, Jamestown, Burlington; Rookie – Bradenton

Pitcher Bob Sebra, in his third major league season.

FACTS ABOUT THE OLYMPIC STADIUM

Location: 4545 Pierre de Coubertin
Capacity: 59,119
Playing surface: artificial turf and roof
1987 day games: 21 (+28 away)
       night games: 60 (+53 away)
1987 ticket prices: $1 to $11.50
Radio: CFCF 600AM, CKAC (Fr.) 730 AM
TV: CBMT (6), CBFT (Fr.Ch2)

Ballpark details

After eight years at Jarry Park, the Expos moved to the $770m Olympic Stadium, in the east of Montreal by the St Lawrence River, in 1977. The 50-ton Kelvar canvas retractable roof, supported by a 552ft concrete and steel mast, was eventually fitted (eleven years late) during the early part of the 1987 Major League season despite a further delay from a fire. The roof takes about forty-five minutes to raise or lower and will surely improve conditions for players and spectators alike. The stadium has excellent access by subway, but there is little ballpark atmosphere about the cavernous, multi-use bowl.

Below: Third baseman Tim Wallach, who hit a home run in his first ML at-bat in 1980.
Right: Montreal's back up catcher, Jeff Reed.

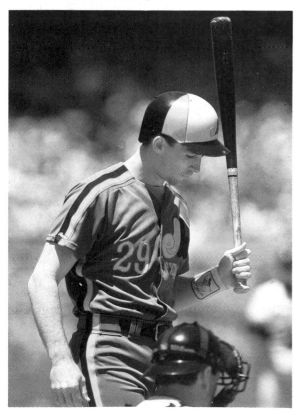

MONTREAL EXPOS in 1987

Manager: Buck Rodgers, 3rd yr with Expos, 6th yr in majors, W-286 L-262.
Expos in '86: W-78 L-83 .484 finished 29½ games behind NY Mets.
NL rankings: batting 5th, pitching 6th.

Montreal's morale took a battering in the off-season with the loss of a major sponsor (who claimed the Expos' market appeal is only in Quebec), and one of its best players, relief pitcher Jeff Reardon. Judging by the indifferent play of spring training, the weak-hitting Expos need more than the return of free agent Tim Raines (who missed the first month of the season by not resigning in time) for the team to fulfil its potential.

Pitching: Apart from top prospect Floyd Youmans, Neal Heaton and Lary Sorensen, the staff of Jay Tibbs, Bob Sebra, Andy McGaffigan, Bob McClure, Randy StClaire, Curt Brown, rookie Mike Smith, and Tim Burke does not look strong enough, even if they all stay healthy.

Catcher: Back-ups Jeff Reed and Dave Engle may see plenty of action if Mike Fitzgerald's injury luck does not improve.

Infielders: Star shortstop Hubie Brooks' injured wrist broke up the solid infield with Andres Galarraga, Vance Law and Tim Wallach, but rookie reserve Casey Candaele is thought a star in the making.

Outfielders: Tim Raines, base stealer Mitch Webster and Herm Winningham on the cold, hard, 'tapis artificiel'.

Leading reserves: Tom Foley, Reid Nichols.

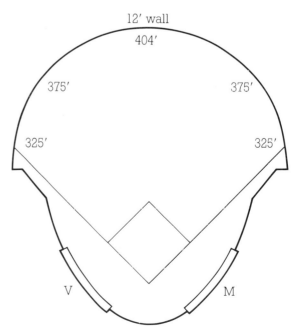

Club name: NEW YORK METS

League/Division: National, East

Postal address: William A. Shea Stadium,
Roosevelt Ave & 126th Street,
Flushing, New York 11368,
USA

History of franchise: New York Mets formed 1962

Won East Div. (since 1969): 1969, 1973, 1986

Won NL: 1969, 1973, 1986

Won World Series: 1969, 1986

Position in div. 1982 to 1986: 6th, 6th, 2nd, 2nd, 1st

1987 spring training site: Al Lang Stadium, St Petersburg, Florida (shared with St Louis Cardinals)

1987 Minor League farm club teams: AAA – Tidewater; AA – Jackson; A – Lynchburg, Columbia, Little Falls; Rookie – Kingsport

Below: Relief pitcher Jesse Orosco.
Right: Outfielder Darryl Strawberry.

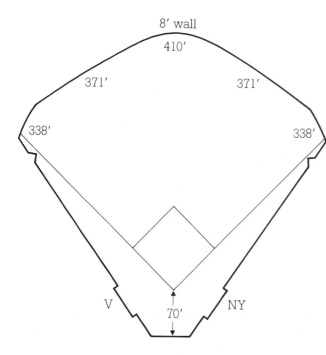

8' wall
410'
371'   371'
338'   338'
V   NY
70'

FACTS ABOUT SHEA STADIUM
Location: Roosevelt Avenue and 126th Street
Capacity: 55,601
Playing surface: grass
1987 day games: 28 (+28 away)
    night games: 53 (+53 away)
1987 ticket prices: $4 to $10
Radio: WHN 1050 AM
TV/cable: WOR(9)/SportsChannel

Ballpark details
The Mets spent their first two years losing at the Polo Grounds, and then moved to miserable Shea Stadium, where the swirling, chilly winds and the noisy jets taking off from nearby La Guardia airport gave them new reasons for making mistakes, until midway through the 1969 season. The stadium was built on landfill in Flushing Meadow, known in the 1920s as Fish-hook Murphy's Dump, so it is not surprising that the grass field is said to have the poorest drainage in the National League. Shea Stadium is not in the best part of New York City by any means, and some visitors may find watching a ballgame intimidating as well.

NEW YORK METS in 1987

Manager: Dave Johnson, 4th yr with Mets, 4th yr in majors, W-296 L-190.

Mets in '86: W-108 L-54 .667 21½ games ahead of division.

NL rankings: batting 1st, pitching 1st.

Every year, most forecasters find it hard to look past the defending champions, and this season's Mets are no exception. They have stars every-where and a farm system that keeps sending up young talent. However, no team has won con-secutive World Series since 1977, and there are good reasons why the Mets may fail in 1987.

Besides letting free agent and Series MVP Ray Knight go to the Orioles, Darryl Strawberry is unhappy at the club, while key relief pitcher Roger McDowell missed the first couple of months because of a hernia operation and starter Bob Ojeda was injured in May and out for the season. Most damaging of all to the team and the club's image and morale was the loss of superstar pitcher Dwight Gooden, on drugs rehabilitation from cocaine until June.

If that was not enough, the team's arrogant play in 1986 antagonised the rest of the league's play-ers and fans so much that this season each match-up has been like playing the NLCS every week. By the dog days of August, the strain of 'Mets v. The Rest' may be telling.

Pitching: Starters Sid Fernandez, Ron Darling and Rick Aguilera are fine pitchers but may pay for the extra work. This has a ripple-on effect for Jesse Orosco, rookie Randy Myers, Doug Sisk, injured David Cone, Terry Leach and rookie John Mitchell.

Catcher: Gary Carter's suspect knees and throw-ing arm must hold out for the season as his leadership is vital. Rookie Barry Lyons is a compe-tent back-up.

Infielders: All-Star Keith Hernandez, Wally Back-man or Tim Teufel, and Howard Johnson risk being exposed by the weak bat of shortstop Rafael Santana with Bill Almon in the platoon.

Outfielders: Kevin McReynolds, Mookie Wilson, and All-Star Darryl Strawberry are kept on their toes by last season's hot bat Len Dykstra.

Leading reserves: Lee Mazilli, and rookie Dave Magadan.

Above: Pitcher Dwight Gooden was 1984 NL Rookie of Year and NL All-Star 1984, 1986.
Right: Catcher Gary Carter, eight times NL All-Star.

Club name: PHILADELPHIA PHILLIES
League/Division: National, East
Postal address: Veterans Stadium, PO Box 7575,
Philadelphia, Pennsylvania
19101, USA
History of franchise: Philadelphia Phillies
formed 1883
Won East Div. (since 1969): 1976, 77, 78, 80, 83
Won NL (since 1900): 1915, 50, 80, 83
Won World Series: 1980
Position in div. 1982 to 1986: 2nd, 1st, 4th, 5th,
2nd
1987 spring training site: Jack Russell Stadium,
Clearwater, Florida
1987 Minor League farm club teams: AAA –
Williamsport; AA – Reading; A – Clearwater,
Spartanburg, Utica

Above Puerto Rican infielder Luis Aguayo.

Right: Outfielder Glenn Wilson, NL All-Star 1985.

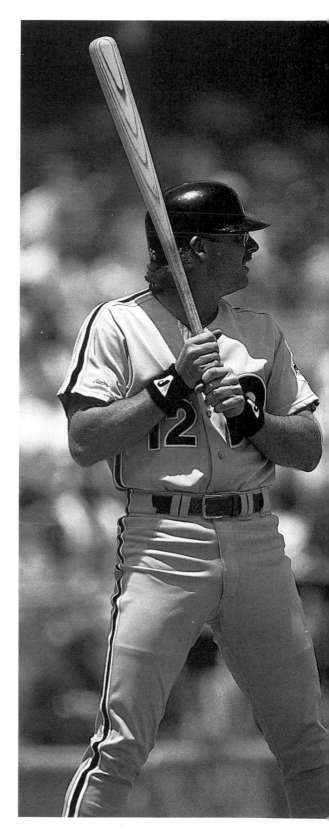

FACTS ABOUT VETERANS STADIUM

Location: Broad Street & Pattirson Avenue
Capacity: 64,538
Playing surface: artificial turf
1987 day games: 18 (+29 away)
      night games: 63 (+52 away)
1987 ticket prices: $4 to $9
Radio: WCAU 1210 AM
TV/cable: WTAF(29)/Prism

Ballpark details

The Phillies had been promised a new stadium on a fourteen-acre site beside the Delaware River for many years, but by the time all the delays and disruptions had been sorted out, the cost had almost doubled to $50m. Veterans Stadium shares its site with two other famous sporting venues, massive JFK Stadium and The Spectrum.

Although the dual-use stadium has good views and access for spectators, it is a pretty heartless place, with fans who have only recently given Mike Schmidt the credit he deserves.

The first ball for the opening game in April 1971 was dropped by helicopter, and since then the Phillies have made the mode of transport used for bringing the first ball to the stadium on Opening Day an increasingly bizarre event.

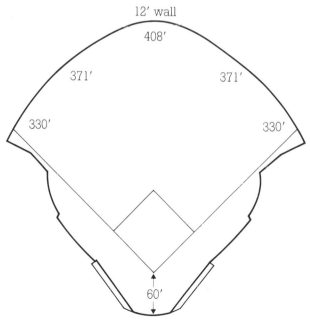

Right: Dominican second baseman Juan Samuel.

Far right: Third baseman Rick Schu played well when Mike Schmidt was injured.

PHILADELPHIA PHILLIES in 1987

Manager: John Felske, 3rd yr with Phillies. Fired 18 June, replaced by Lee Elia.
Phillies in '86: W-86 L-75 .534 finished 21½ games behind NY Mets.
NL rankings: batting 7th, pitching 7th.

Philadelphia has plenty of batting power and speed around the field, but the pitching is not what it was in Steve Carlton's heyday. In the off-season, the club did well to sign free agent catcher Lance Parrish, but in order to win the division they may have done better to get his more famous Detroit teammate, pitcher Jack Morris.

Pitching: Shane Rawley, Don Carman, Kevin Gross are either recovering from injury, disaffected with the manager, or both. Bruce Ruffin and Dan Schatzedar help to keep the runs down long enough for good relievers Kent Tekulve, Tom Hume, rookie Wally Ritchie and Steve Bedrosian to do their work.

Catcher: AL All-Star Lance Parrish cost $800,000 (plus incentives) but will seem worth it if he stays healthy. John Russell and Darren Daulton are in reserve.

Infielders: Von Hayes, Juan Samuel and All-Star Mike Schmidt usually provide enough punch to cover for shortstop Steve Jeltz's weak hitting. Rick Schu is the infield cover.

Outfielders: Glenn Wilson, Milt Thompson, and hot batter/poor fielder Mike Easler.

Leading reserves: Luis Aguayo, and Greg Gross.

Club name: PITTSBURGH PIRATES
League/Division: National, East
Postal address: Three River Stadium, 600 Stadium Circle, Pittsburgh, Pennsylvania 15212, USA
History of franchise: Pittsburgh Pirates formed 1887 (celebrating centenary year)
Won East Div. (since 1969): 1970, 71, 72, 74, 75, 79
Won NL (since 1900): 1901, 02, 03, 09, 25, 27, 60, 71, 79
Won World Series: 1909, 25, 60, 71, 79
Position in div. 1982 to 1986: 4th, 2nd, 6th, 6th, 6th
1987 spring training site: McKechnie Field, Bradenton, Florida
1987 Minor League farm club teams: AAA – Vancouver; AA – Harrisburg; A – Salem, Macon, Watertown; Rookie – Bradenton

Left: Pitcher Dorn Taylor made his ML debut with the Pirates in 1987.

FACTS ABOUT THREE RIVER STADIUM

Location: 600 Stadium Circle
Capacity: 58,438
Playing surface: artificial turf
1987 day games: 17 (+28 away)
      night games: 64 (+53 away)
1987 ticket prices: $2.50 to $9.50
Radio: KDKA 1020 AM
TV/cable: KDKA(2)/TCI

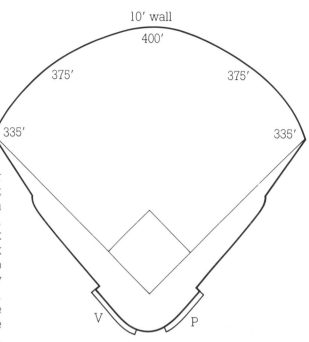

Ballpark details

The Pirates had been playing at Forbes Field for over thirty years when a new stadium was first mentioned. A site was chosen in a rundown area on the north bank of the confluence of the Ohio, Allegheny and Monongahela Rivers. But it took another decade of planning and building work bedevilled by labour disputes before the club played its first game in the $55m stadium in July 1970. Although the site is boxed in by freeways, the relatively poor access deters all but the diehard fans. Some find it easier to travel to the stadium by riverboat. After the Second World War, entertainer Bing Crosby was a co-owner for some years.

Below: Reliable second baseman Johnny Ray, 1982 NL Rookie of the Year, dives for the base.

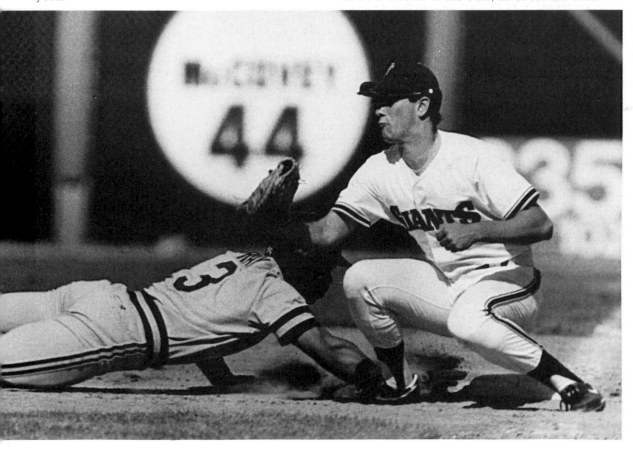

PITTSBURGH PIRATES in 1987

Manager: Jim Leyland, 2nd yr with Pirates, 2nd yr in majors, W-64 L-98.

Pirates in '86: W-64 L-98 .395 finished 44 games behind the NY Mets.

NL rankings: batting 10th, pitching 8th.

Manager Jim Leyland expects Pittsburgh's youngsters to be better than the 1986 team, but that is not saying much. The new management has halved the financial losses to about $4m by getting rid of some expensive stars, and investing in a youth programme which it is hoped will bring dividends next season. The problem will be to encourage Pittsburgh fans to attend in sufficient numbers to pay the wages while the players are learning.

36-year-old utilityman infielder Jim Morrison.

Pitching: Starters Bob Kipper, portly Rick Reuschel, Doug Drabek, Brian Fisher, rookie Dorn Taylor and the unfortunately named Bob Walk, present a thankless task to relievers Don Robinson, and rookies John Smiley, Logan Easley and Hipolita Pena.

Catcher: Mike LaValliere made a good start at taking over from the great Tony Pena, and has Junior Ortiz to back him up.

Infielders: Sid Bream, Johnny Ray, and Jim Morrison are hard-hitting basemen who make up for shortstop Rafael Belliard in a solid infield.

Outfielders: Bobby Bonilla, Barry Bonds, and Andy Van Slyke get plenty of work in the deep, with R. J. Reynolds, Mike Diaz, John Cangelosi, and Terry Harper when they need a well-earned rest. In these modern, artificial turf stadiums the ball is said to bounce around like marble thrown in an empty bath.

Club name: ST LOUIS CARDINALS

League/Division: National, East

Postal address: Busch Memorial Stadium, 250 Stadium Plaza, St Louis, Missouri 63102, USA

History of franchise: St Louis Cardinals (1876–77, 1885–86), present club formed 1892

Won East Div. (since 1969): 1982, 1985

Won NL (since 1900): 1926, 28, 30, 31, 34, 42, 43, 44, 46, 64, 67, 68, 82, 85

Won World Series: 1926, 31, 42, 44, 46, 64, 67, 82

Position in div. 1982 to 1986: 1st, 4th, 3rd, 1st, 3rd

1987 spring training site: Al Lang Stadium, St Petersburg, Florida (shared with New York Mets)

1987 Minor League farm club teams: AAA – Louisville; AA – Little Rock; A – St Petersburg, Erie, Savannah, Springfield; Rookie – Johnson City

Below: Northampton born pitcher Danny Cox has played well again in 1987.

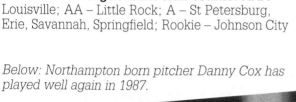

Above: 28-year-old pitcher Pat Perry played for seven minor league teams before making his NL debut for St Louis in 1985.

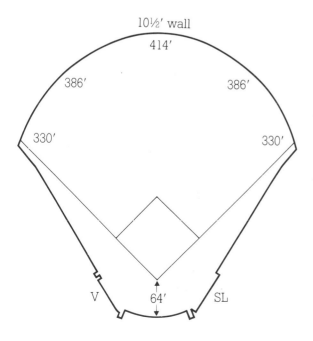

FACTS ABOUT BUSCH MEMORIAL STADIUM

Location: Broadway, Walnut Street, Stadium Plaza and Spruce Street.
Capacity: 50,100
Playing surface: artificial turf
1987 day games: 22 (+32 away)
    night games: 59 (+49 away)
1987 ticket prices: $4 to $9.50
Radio: KMOX 1120 AM
TV/cable: KSDK(5)/Cencom

Ballpark details

In the early 1960s, businessmen were keen to have a sports stadium built in a central part of St Louis to help revitalise the area's flagging economy. Brewing giant Anheuser-Busch guaranteed $5m to start the project and soon a city referendum voted in favour of clearing a thirty-acre site near the Mississippi River.

On a cold night in May 1966, two years after building started, the Cardinals played their first game in the stadium. The range of temperatures that fans must endure during the season is one of the few disadvantages of this clean, modern stadium near the massive Gateway Arch. Only two months after freezing at the opening, spectators were sweltering in temperatures of 105°F at the All-Star game.

ST LOUIS CARDINALS in 1987
Manager: Whitey Herzog, 8th yr with Cardinals, 15th yr in majors, W-991 L-849.
Cardinals in '86: W-79 L-82 .491 finished 28½ games behind NY Mets.
NL rankings: batting 12th, pitching 4th.

In 1986, the Cards hit only fifty-eight home runs in a woeful reverse for their speedy, top-rated batting line-up from 1985. With a stronger squad available this year the club would seem to need only an average year with the bat to win the division from the Cubs. Manager Herzog won his 1,000th game in the Major Leagues in April with a St Louis team that typifies the NL running style of play.
Pitching: Starters Danny Cox, Bob Forsch, Tim Conroy, Joe Magrane, Lee Tunnell, Bill Dawley, and Pat Perry set up the game for Rick Horton and last season's Rookie of the Year, Todd Worrell, in relief.

The staff's character was tested for three months following the freak accident to ace left-hander John Tudor who broke a knee in a needless collision while watching a game from the dugout.
Catcher: Tony Pena, acquired from Pittsburgh, is probably one of the top catchers in the league so it was a cruel blow when he broke his thumb in his first game against the Pirates. Steve Lake played well in his absence.

Far left: Relief pitcher Todd Worrell was 1986 Rookie of the Year, and Fireman of the Year with 36 saves.

Left: Busch Memorial Stadium, scene of the 1985 World Series.

Above: 32-year-old shortstop Osborne Earl Smith, the finest fielder in the NL. Traded to St Louis from San Diego for Garry Templeton in 1982.

Infielders: Jack Clark, Tommy Herr, and Terry Pendleton concentrate on their batting while All-Star shortstop Ozzie 'The Wizard' Smith proves he is still one of the all-time great fielders.
Outfielders: Rookie Jim Lindeman, Willie McGee, and base stealing expert Vince Coleman are as fast as any combination in the league.
Leading reserves: Curt Ford, Jose Oquendo, Tito Landrum and rookie Rod Booker.

Club name: ATLANTA BRAVES
League/Division: National, West
Postal address: Atlanta-Fulton County Stadium, PO Box 4064, Atlanta, Georgia 30302, USA
History of franchise: Boston Braves 1876–1952, Milwaukee Braves 1953–65, Atlanta Braves since 1966
Honours won in Atlanta:
Won West Div. (since 1969): 1969, 1982
Yet to win NL or World Series since moving to Atlanta
Position in div. 1982 to 1986: 1st, 2nd, 2nd, 5th, 6th
1987 spring training site: Municipal Stadium, West Palm Beach, Florida (shared with Montreal Expos)
1987 Minor League farm club teams: AAA – Richmond; AA – Greenville; A – Durham, Sumter; Rookie – Pulaski, Bradenton, Idaho Falls

FACTS ABOUT ATLANTA-FULTON COUNTY STADIUM

Location: on Capitol Avenue at junction of Interstate Highways 20, 75 & 85
Capacity: 52,003
Playing surface: grass
1987 day games: 30 (+20 away)
night games: 51 (+61 away)
1987 ticket prices: $3 to $8.50
Radio: WSB 750 AM
TV/cable: WTBS (17) Superstation

Ballpark details

In April 1964 work started on an $18m dual-use stadium in a rundown area of south-central Atlanta, only a mile from the State Capitol. Almost two years later, the Braves had moved in from Milwaukee to bring Major League baseball to Atlanta.

The stadium was the scene for one of baseball's most significant moments of recent years, when, at 9.07pm on 8 April 1974, in the fourth inning of a game against Los Angeles, Henry 'Hank the Hammer' Aaron hit his 715th career home run over the left field fence to break Babe Ruth's record.

For the most part, not even the summer thunderstorms that afflict the area have been able to put a winning spark into the team, whose games have been enlivened by Chief Nokahoma and his wigwam out in the bleachers.

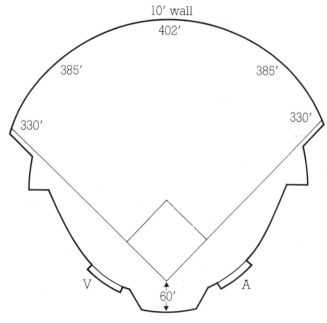

Left: Braves on the basepaths prefer the leisurely home run trot to stealing bases.
Above: Dale Murphy, NL MVP 1982 and 1983.

33

ATLANTA BRAVES in 1987

Manager: Chuck Tanner, 2nd yr with Braves, 18th yr in majors, W-1,271 L-1,262.

Braves in '86: W-72 L-89 .447 finished 23½ games behind Houston.

NL rankings: batting 10th, pitching 10th.

Last season was yet another the Braves would like to forget. Ace relief pitcher Bruce Sutter had a long injury, All-Star Dale Murphy had an off year, and the farm system was no help at all.

With Sutter still out in 1987, the best straws to clutch at are that manager Chuck Tanner knows what it is like to be successful, and that by losing a number of overpaid veterans Atlanta has helped bring down the 1987 Major League wage bill by an average $23,500 to $415,000 per player.

Below: Outfielder Dion James played 150 games for the Brewers (AL) before being traded to Atlanta in 1987.
Inset: Manager Chuck Tanner.

Pitching: Starters Rick Mahler, Zane Smith, Randy O'Neal and David Palmer and resigned free agent Doyle Alexander are on a hiding to nothing in Atlanta's home run heaven, and rarely put relievers Jeff Dedmon, veteran Gene Garber, Jim Acker, Paul Assenmacher, or Charlie Puleo in a favourable position.

Catcher: Home run hitter Ozzie Virgil is backed up by veteran Bruce Benedict.

Infielders: Gerald Perry, consistent Ken Oberkfell, and young shortstop Andres Thomas are platooned with Glenn Hubbard and Rafael Ramirez.

Outfielders: Revitalised All-Star slugger Dale Murphy, Dion James and Ken Griffey revel at the plate in Atlanta, and have reserves such as Albert Hall, veteran Graig Nettles, Gary Roenicke and Ted Simmons. Dion James hit a dove with base hit at Shea Stadium in April. The fatal deflection turned an easy catch into a double, from which he scored. In 1983, Dave Winfield (Yankees), hit a seagull with a throw during practice at Toronto.

Club name: CINCINNATI REDS
League/Division: National, West
Postal address: 100 Riverfront Stadium,
Cincinnati, Ohio 45202, USA
History of franchise: Cincinnati Reds (1876–1880), present club formed 1890
Won West Div. (since 1969): 1970, 72, 73, 75, 76, 79
Won NL (since 1900): 1919, 39, 40, 61, 70, 72, 75, 76
Won World Series: 1919, 40, 75, 76
Position in div. 1982 to 1986: 6th, 6th, 5th, 2nd, 2nd
1987 spring training site: Al Lopez Field, Tampa, Florida
1987 Minor League farm club teams: AAA – Nashville; AA – Vermont; A – Cedar Rapids, Tampa; Rookie – Billings, Sarasota

Third baseman Buddy Bell has played over 2,200 games in 16 seasons. Traded from Texas (AL) in 1985.

FACTS ABOUT RIVERFRONT STADIUM

Location: downtown Cincinnati, Pete Rose Way to Ohio River, and Walnut St to Broadway
Capacity: 59,392
Playing surface: artificial turf
1987 day games: 27 (+29 away)
      night games: 54 (+52 away)
1987 ticket prices: $3.50 to $8.50
Radio: WLW 700 AM
TV: WLWT (5)

Ballpark details

Riverfront Stadium cost $48m and was built on the north bank of the Ohio River, beside the road bridge that crosses into Kentucky. The first game was played in June 1970, and the team soon found it to their liking, as the 'Big Red Machine' won the National League that season and rolled to four more titles in the next six years. Cincinnati has always attracted its baseball fans from a wide catchment area, with season ticket holders travelling from up to 200 miles for games. The amiable fans and pleasant surroundings help make Riverfront one of the best of the modern dual-use stadiums for baseball, and some think it would be even better if they replaced the artificial turf with grass.

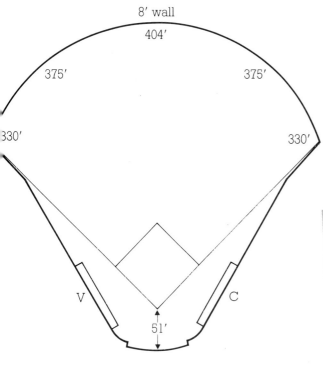

CINCINNATI REDS in 1987

Manager: Pete Rose, 4th yr (as manager) with Reds, 4th yr in majors, W-194 L-170.
Reds in '86: W-86 L-76 .531 finished 10 games behind Houston.
NL rankings: batting 5th, pitching 9th.

This is the year when Pete Rose's managing preference for experience over youth will end. The team is packed with powerful long ball hitters and has good relief pitchers. The starting rotation prevented the club winning the division but some wonder if the team's chances were affected by Pete's philosophy. Last season the club made a dreadful start and were left behind by May. This year, the Reds tucked in with the leaders and showed the Giants that they would not have it all their own way.

Pitching: Starters Bill Gullickson, Ted Power, Rob Murphy, Guy Hoffman, and less injured Mario Soto hope that the 'Red Menace' bats will paper over the cracks in the rotation long enough for relievers John Franco, Ron Robinson and Frank Williams to finish the game.
Catcher: Bo Diaz helps the pitchers, as a good catcher should.
Infielders: Terry Francona, Ron Oester, young Barry Larkin, and veteran Buddy Bell at third base will always be overshadowed by the big three behind them.
Outfielders: Dave Parker, the game's next superstar Eric Davis, and fellow base stealer Kal Daniels are kept on their toes by young Tracy Jones.
Leading reserves: Veteran Dave Concepcion, Nick Esasky, young Kurt Stillwell and a certain pinch-hitter with a career record 4,256 hits who became eligible to play from 15 May, Pete Rose.

Below: Awesome 'F', outfielder Eric Davis could dominate the game for the next decade.
Right: Pitcher Ted Power, signed by LA in 1976 played in only 17 ML games before being traded to the Reds in 1982.

Club name: HOUSTON ASTROS

League/Division: National, West
Postal address: The Astrodome, PO Box 288,
Houston, Texas 77001, USA
History of franchise: Houston Astros formed
1962
Won West Div. (since 1969): 1980, 1986
Yet to win NL or World Series
Position in div. 1982 to 1986: 5th, 3rd, 2nd, 3rd,
1st
1987 spring training site: Osceola County
Stadium, Kissimmee, Florida
1987 Minor League farm club teams: AAA –
Tucson; AA – Columbus; A – Osceola, Auburn,
Asheville; Rookie – Sarasota

FACTS ABOUT THE ASTRODOME

Location: Kirby and Interstate Loop 610
Capacity: 45,000
Playing surface: artificial turf and roof
1987 day games: 20 (+31 away)
 night games: 61 (+50 away)
1987 ticket prices: $3 to $8.50
Radio: KTRH 740 AM
TV/cable: KTXH (20)/HSE

Ballpark details

After three seasons suffering the searing heat, rain
and thunderstorms, strong winds and mosquitoes
in Colt Stadium, the club moved just 400 yards
across the car park into what Texans called the
'Eighth Wonder of the World', the fully air-
conditioned $32m Harris County Domed Stadium
or Astrodome. The first game, in April 1965, was
attended by US President Lyndon B. Johnson.

Originally, the Astrodome had a grass field, but
when fielders complained that they could not see
the ball in the glare, the transparent dome was
painted and the grass died. The first of its artificial
turf playing surfaces was rolled out the following
year. The playing field is about 25 feet below
ground level which gives a vertical clearance of
208 feet. The only player to hit a ball into the roof
has been Mike Schmidt, in 1974.

The multi-use Astrodome had a $42m facelift in
1982 but even that has not made it a true ballpark
for baseball.

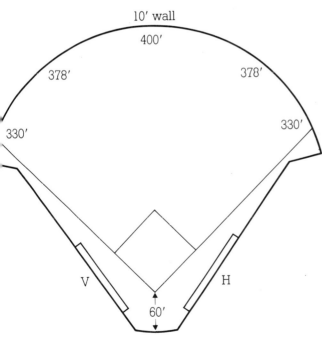

*Right: Mexican relief pitcher Aurelio Lopez signed
with the Astros in 1986.*

*Far right: Outfielder Jose Cruz made his ML debut
for St Louis in 1970.*

HOUSTON ASTROS in 1987

Manager: Hal Lanier, 2nd yr with Astros, 2nd yr in majors, W-96 L-66.

Astros in '86: W-96 L-66 .593 won West division by 10 games.

NL rankings: batting 4th, pitching 2nd.

By winning the division in his first season, Manager of the Year Hal Lanier must have wondered if managing in the majors was as hard as they said. He is likely to find out this year, as the club did not use the off-season to sign the catcher, big hitters, or left-handed relief pitcher it needed.

Pitching: Two of Houston's pitchers are worth the price of admission whenever they start, Mike Scott and Nolan Ryan. Making up the rotation and the bullpen are Jim Deshaies, Larry Andersen, Danny Darwin, Bob Knepper, and relievers Aurelio Lopez and Dave Meads. One of last season's stars Charlie Kerfeld, was sent down to the minors to lose weight and recover his speed.

Catcher: Previously weak thrower and batter, Alan Ashby was given a boost when the club failed to sign Tony Pena or Rich Gedman.

Infielders: Glenn Davis, Bill Doran, Denny Walling and shortstops Craig Reynolds and Dickie Thon (who has eye trouble) must hit well again this season as there is little depth to the infield squad.

Outfielders: Kevin Bass, star hitter Billy Hatcher, and Jose Cruz have Terry Puhl, Davey Lopes, Paul Householder and Mark Bailey waiting in the wings.

Outfielder Billy Hatcher has had his best season since being traded from the Cubs in 1985.

Club name: LOS ANGELES DODGERS
League/Division: National, West
Postal address: Dodger Stadium, 1000 Elysian
Park Ave., Los Angeles,
California 90012, USA
History of franchise: Brooklyn Dodgers 1890–
1957, Los Angeles Dodgers since 1958
Won West Div. (since 1969): 1974, 77, 78, 81, 83,
85
Won NL since moving to LA: 1959, 63, 65, 66,
74, 77, 78, 81
Won World Series in LA: 1959, 63, 65, 81
Position in div. 1982 to 1986: 2nd, 1st, 4th, 1st,
5th
1987 spring training site: Holman Field, Vero
Beach, Florida
1987 Minor League farm club teams: AAA –
Albuquerque; AA – San Antonio; A – Bakersfield,
Vero Beach; Rookie – Great Falls, Sarasota

*Reliable second baseman,
Steve Sax, was 1982 NL
Rookie of the Year and
NL All-Star 1982, 1983
and 1986.*

FACTS ABOUT DODGER STADIUM

Location: 1000 Eylsian Park Avenue
Capacity: 56,000
Playing surface: grass
1987 day games: 21 (+28 away)
     night games: 60 (+53 away)
1987 ticket prices: $4 to $7
Radio: KABC 790AM, KWKW (Spanish) 1300 AM
TV/cable: KTTV (11)/Dodgervision

Ballpark details

When the Dodgers fled west from Brooklyn they played for four years in the LA Memorial Coliseum, where they averaged almost 2 million fans a season. Meanwhile, work progressed on the club's own ballpark in Chavez Ravine not far from Hollywood. The gulches and gullies carved by the Los Angeles River made it a difficult 300-acre site to drain and reshape. However, the effort was well worth it, as clean, colour-coded, Dodger Stadium is arguably the best ballpark in the Major Leagues. In the twenty-five years since the first game in April 1962, over 65 million fans have enjoyed the sun, the food, the view of the San Gabriel Mountains in the background, and spotting movie stars in the crowd.

The only disappointing aspect is that there are only twenty-one day games in 1987, and that many fans leave after the seventh inning to avoid the traffic jam on the freeway.

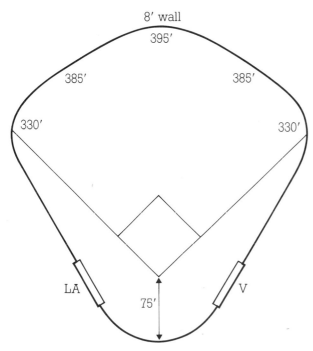

LOS ANGELES DODGERS in 1987

Manager: Tom Lasorda, 11th yr with Dodgers, 11th yr in majors, W-853 L-716.
Dodgers in '86: W-73 L-89 .451 finished 23 games behind Houston.
NL rankings: batting 9th, pitching 5th.

No franchise rebuilds a team quicker than the Dodgers even if the farm system is not what it was. If the team's three or four superstars stay fit, Los Angeles should do well. However, the team's sloppy fielding and poor bullpen suggest the problems may not go away so easily this time. The forced resignation of seventy-year-old Vice President Al Campanis for remarks he made on television on the public debate about blacks in baseball management, unsettled the club during the spring.

A novel experience for the Dodgers this season has been travelling to away games on scheduled flights. In previous years the Dodgers have had their own plane or have chartered one.

Pitching: Ace starter Fernando Valenzuela has probably been the best left-hander in the majors for the past six seasons, and he shares the rotation with Rick Honeycutt and right-handers Orel Hershiser and Bob Welch, Contesting the remaining starting slot and the relief pitching are Ken Howell, rookie Brian Holton, Alejandro Pena, Matt Young, and Tim Leary.

Catcher: Mike Scioscia, a great catcher who bats well too, has Alex Trevino in support.

Infielders: Franklin Stubbs, Steve Sax, Phil Garner and Mariano Duncan look frail at best, with Micky Hatcher in reserve. Aussie baseball fans will be looking for rookie infielder Craig Shipley, from Sydney, who played a dozen games in 1986.

Outfielders: With superstar Pedro Guerrero's knee injury fully recovered, the deep field looks better. Mike Marshall, Ken Landreaux, and rookie Tracy Woodson are pressed by Ralph Bryant, Danny Heep and John Shelby.

Above left: Injury prone catcher Mike Scioscia has played over 700 games for LA since his ML debut in 1980.

Above right: First baseman Franklin Stubbs, 1982 College All-America, was selected in the first round of the 1982 free agent draft.

Left: Beautiful Dodger Stadium, arguably the best ballpark in the major leagues.

Club name: SAN DIEGO PADRES

League/Division: National, West

Postal address: San Diego Stadium, 9449 Friars Road, San Diego, California 92108, USA

History of franchise: San Diego Padres formed 1969

Won West Div. (since 1969): 1984

Won NL: 1984

Yet to win World Series

Position in div. 1982 to 1986: 4th, 4th, 1st, 3rd, 4th

1987 spring training site: Desert Sun Stadium, Yuma, Arizona

1987 Minor League farm club teams: AAA – Las Vegas; AA – Wichita; A – Reno, Charleston, Spokane

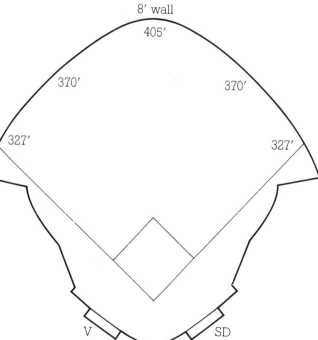

FACTS ABOUT JACK MURPHY STADIUM

Location: 9449 Friars Road
Capacity: 58,433
Playing surface: grass
1987 day games: 24 (+25 away)
     night games: 57 (+56 away)
1987 ticket prices: $3.50 to $8
Radio: KFMB 760AM, XEXX (Spanish) 1420AM
TV/cable: KUSI (51)/Cox Cable

Ballpark details

In the mid-1960s, the San Diego city council wanted to build a large, dual-use $28m stadium in the hope of attracting professional baseball and football franchises. Once approved in a local referendum, work started in Mission Valley to divert the San Diego River from its course to the Pacific Ocean. The stadium, opened in 1967, was named after the newspaper sports editor who had campaigned for the facility for many years.

The Padres took their name from the nearby eighteenth-century Franciscan mission and joined the National League in 1969, but despite its NL pennant in 1984, the team has yet to make the most of playing in an attractive ballpark with almost perfect weather conditions. Perhaps indicative of this is the fact that one of the club's most famous figures is the 'San Diego Chicken', which visits other ballparks during the season and has inspired many imitators. Being on the West coast, fans can watch action from earlier games to the East, on the giant video screen.

Left: Veteran relief pitcher Rich 'Goose' Gossage.
Below: Rookie catcher Benito Santiago.

SAN DIEGO PADRES in 1987

Manager: Larry Bowa, 1st yr with the Padres, 1st yr in majors. (Las Vegas, AAA Pacific Coast League 1986.)

Padres in '86: W-74 L-88 .457 finished 22 games behind Houston.

NL rankings: batting 2nd, pitching 11th.

Rookie manager Larry Bowa's positive, aggressive attitude will either prove to be just what the club's younger players need, or out of place in sleepy, sunny, southern California.

The team's uphill task is to get the weak pitchers to concede fewer runs so that the potentially good runners and batters have a better chance to win the game. It has not helped the team's preparation to have so much gossip about the club's ownership. Joan Kroc, widow of the founder of McDonald's Hamburgers, Ray Kroc, may sell the franchise this season. Early season rumours favoured George Argyros (who would have to sell the Seattle Mariners) but injured veteran first baseman Steve Garvey is part of a consortium keen to buy a major league club.

Below: Shortstop Garry Templeton; NL All-Star 1977 and 1985.

Above: Hard hitting outfielder John Kruk – a Padres success.

Right: Giants pitcher Mark Grant.

Pitching: The rotation of Eric Show, Storm Davis, Andy Hawkins, Ed Whitson and Dave Dravecky looks weak and needs strengthening. It is unlikely to hand much worth defending to relievers Lance McCullers, disaffected veteran Rich 'Goose' Gossage, Craig Lefferts and Greg Booker.

Catcher: Rookie Benito Santiago is thought to be a tremendous prospect, and has a great throwing arm. Bruce Bochy is his back up.

Infielders: Tim Flannery, basestealer Joey Cora, Garry Templeton, and shortstop Kevin Mitchell from the Mets do not look as impressive as the outfielders.

Outfielders: John Kruk, Stan Jefferson and the club's many outfielders have the honour of being on the field with Golden Glove, All-Star, basestealing, superman Tony Gwynn.

Leading reserves: Carmelo Martinez, Luis Salazar, Shane Mack, Marvell Wynne, James Steels, and the curiously named Randy Ready.

Club name: SAN FRANCISCO GIANTS
League/Division: National, West
Postal address: Candlestick Park, San Francisco, California 94124, USA
History of franchise: New York Giants 1883–1957, moved to San Francisco 1958
Won West Div. (since 1969): 1971
Won NL since moving to SF: 1962
Yet to win NL or World Series since moving to SF.
Position in div. 1982 to 1986: 3rd, 5th, 6th, 6th, 3rd
1987 spring training site: Scottsdale Stadium, Scottsdale, Arizona
1987 Minor League farm club teams: AAA – Phoenix; AA – Shreveport; A – Fresno, Clinton, Everett; Rookie – Pocatello

FACTS ABOUT CANDLESTICK PARK

Location: Candlestick Point, Bayshore Freeway
Capacity: 58,000
Playing surface: grass
1987 day games: 42 (+23 away)
     night games: 39 (+58 away)
1987 ticket prices: $2.50 to $9
Radio: KNBR 680 AM
TV/cable: KTVU (2)/GiantsVision

Ballpark details

Baseball is known to have been played in San Francisco over 120 years ago so it is surprising that somewhere more suitable was not found for their Major League ballpark than Candlestick Point, on the west side of San Francisco Bay.

When the Giants arrived from New York the team played for two years at Seals Stadium while the first heated open-air dual-use stadium was being built for $24.6m. All too often since it opened in April 1960 the players and the loyal, knowledgeable fans have been tested by fog and cold swirling winds which make night games a particular test of endurance. The $16m renovation in 1971, when artificial turf was laid (then ripped up eight years later), did not improve things much, but at least the new, $4.7m scoreboard has reduced the wind problem.

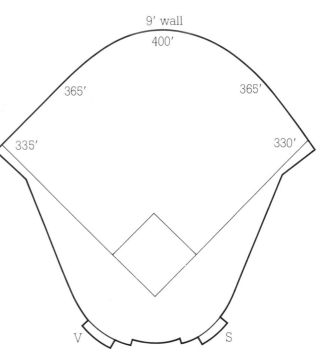

Below: Recent action from Giants v. Braves.
Right: Watching the action from the Giants' dugout.

SAN FRANCISCO GIANTS in 1987
Manager: Roger Craig, 3rd yr with Giants, 5th yr in majors, W-241 L-262.
Giants in '86: W-83 L-79 .512 finished 13 games behind Houston.
NL rankings: batting 7th, pitching 3rd.

Now that Roger Craig has taught everyone on the franchise, from pitchers to tea ladies, how to throw the split-fingered fastball, he can concentrate on keeping his key players fit, protected from the cold night air, and beat Cincinnati and Houston in the division.

The team's achievement in turning from 100-game losers in 1985 into a team that led the West for forty-seven days, despite injuries, counts for little with the players, who remember the team's lack of speed, and finishing thirteen games adrift. After a great spring, things may be different.
Pitching: Right-handers Mike Krukow, Mark Grant, Mike LaCoss, and left-handers Mark Davis, Atlee Hammaker and Kelly Downs are not as impressive as the relievers Jeff Robinson and Scott Garrelts, or Jim Gott.
Catcher: Bob Melvin and Bob Brenly are reliable behind the plate.

Above: Rookie pitcher Kelly Downs grabbed his chance after six years in the minors.

Infielders: Will Clark, young Robby Thompson, Chris Brown, and shortstop Jose Uribe make an extremely impressive but injury prone line-up, with Chris Speier and Mike Aldrete in reserve.
Outfielders: Jeffrey Leonard, unsettled Jamaican Chili Davis and Candy Maldonado add to the inhibiting sight for opposing batters and pitchers.
Leading reserves: Harry Spilman, Eddie Milner (out of the majors for drugs rehabilitation), and veteran Joel Youngblood, whose photograph features anonymously on the cover of *A Guide to Baseball*.

49

NATIONAL LEAGUE PENNANT WINNERS

Year	Club	W.	L.	Pct.	G.A.	Year	Club	W.	L.	Pct.	G.A.
1876	Chicago	52	14	.788	6	1936	New York	92	62	.597	5
1877	Boston	31	17	.646	3	1937	New York	95	57	.625	3
1878	Boston	41	19	.683	4	1938	Chicago	89	63	.586	2
1879	Providence	55	23	.705	6	1939	Cincinnati	97	57	.630	4½
1880	Chicago	67	17	.798	15	1940	Cincinnati	100	53	.654	12
1881	Chicago	56	27	.667	9	1941	Brooklyn	100	54	.649	2½
1882	Chicago	55	29	.655	3	1942	St Louis	106	48	.688	2
1883	Boston	63	35	.643	4	1943	St Louis	105	49	.682	18
1884	Providence	84	28	.750	10½	1944	St Louis	105	49	.682	14½
1885	Chicago	87	25	.777	2	1945	Chicago	98	56	.636	3
1886	Chicago	90	34	.726	2½	1946	a) St Louis	98	58	.628	2
1887	Detroit	79	45	.637	3½	1947	Brooklyn	94	60	.610	5
1888	New York	84	47	.641	9	1948	Boston	91	62	.595	6½
1889	New York	83	43	.659	1	1949	Brooklyn	97	57	.630	1
1890	Brooklyn	86	43	.667	6½	1950	Philadelphia	91	63	.591	2
1891	Boston	87	51	.630	3½	1951	b) New York	98	59	.624	1
1892	Boston	102	48	.680	8½	1952	Brooklyn	96	57	.627	4½
1893	Boston	86	44	.662	4½	1953	Brooklyn	105	49	.682	13
1894	Baltimore	89	39	.695	3	1954	New York	97	57	.630	5
1895	Baltimore	87	43	.669	3	1955	Brooklyn	98	55	.641	13½
1896	Baltimore	90	39	.698	9½	1956	Brooklyn	93	61	.604	1
1897	Boston	93	39	.705	2	1957	Milwaukee	95	59	.617	9
1898	Boston	102	47	.685	6	1958	Milwaukee	92	62	.597	8
1899	Brooklyn	88	42	.677	4	1959	c) Los Angeles	88	68	.564	2
1900	Brooklyn	82	54	.603	4½	1960	Pittsburgh	95	59	.617	7
1901	Pittsburgh	90	49	.647	7½	1961	Cincinnati	93	61	.604	4
1902	Pittsburgh	103	36	.741	27½	1962	d) San Francisco	103	62	.624	1
1903	Pittsburgh	91	49	.650	6½	1963	Los Angeles	99	63	.611	6
1904	New York	106	47	.693	13	1964	St Louis	93	69	.574	1
1905	New York	105	48	.686	9	1965	Los Angeles	97	65	.599	2
1906	Chicago	116	36	.763	20	1966	Los Angeles	95	67	.586	1½
1907	Chicago	107	45	.704	17	1967	St Louis	101	60	.627	10½
1908	Chicago	99	55	.643	1	1968	St Louis	97	65	.599	9
1909	Pittsburgh	110	42	.724	6½	1969	New York (E)	100	62	.617	8
1910	Chicago	104	50	.675	13	1970	Cincinnati (W)	102	60	.630	14½
1911	New York	99	54	.647	7½	1971	Pittsburgh (E)	97	65	.599	7
1912	New York	103	48	.682	10	1972	Cincinnati (W)	95	59	.617	10½
1913	New York	101	51	.664	12½	1973	New York (E)	82	79	.509	1½
1914	Boston	94	59	.614	10½	1974	Los Angeles (W)	102	60	.630	4
1915	Philadelphia	90	62	.592	7	1975	Cincinnati (W)	108	54	.667	20
1916	Brooklyn	94	60	.610	2½	1976	Cincinnati (W)	102	60	.630	10
1917	New York	98	56	.636	10	1977	Los Angeles (W)	98	64	.605	10
1918	Chicago	84	45	.651	10½	1978	Los Angeles (W)	95	67	.586	2½
1919	Cincinnati	96	44	.686	9	1979	Pittsburgh (E)	98	64	.605	2
1920	Brooklyn	93	61	.604	7	1980	Philadelphia (E)	91	71	.562	1
1921	New York	94	59	.614	4	1981	e) Los Angeles (W)	63	47	.573	—
1922	New York	93	61	.604	7	1982	St Louis (E)	92	70	.568	3
1923	New York	95	58	.621	4½	1983	Philadelphia (E)	90	72	.556	6
1924	New York	93	60	.608	1½	1984	San Diego (W)	92	70	.568	12
1925	Pittsburgh	95	58	.621	8½	1985	St Louis (E)	101	61	.623	3
1926	St Louis	89	65	.578	2	1986	New York (E)	108	54	.667	21½
1927	Pittsburgh	94	60	.610	1½	1987					
1928	St Louis	95	59	.617	2						
1929	Chicago	98	54	.645	10½						
1930	St Louis	92	62	.597	2						
1931	St Louis	101	53	.656	13						
1932	Chicago	90	64	.584	4						
1933	New York	91	61	.599	5						
1934	St Louis	95	58	.621	2						
1935	Chicago	100	54	.649	4						

G.A.: Games ahead of second-place club. a) Defeated Brooklyn, two games to none, in playoff. b) Defeated Brooklyn, two games to one, in playoff for pennant. c) Defeated Milwaukee, two games to none, in playoff. d) Defeated Los Angeles, two games to one, in playoff. e) First half 36–21; second half 27–26 of strike-hit season.

NATIONAL LEAGUE REGULAR SEASON RECORDS SINCE 1900

NL TEAM RECORDS
Most wins: 108 Cincinnati 1975, NY 1986
Most defeats: 120 New York 1962
Earliest West Division win: 7 Sept 1975
Earliest East Division win: 17 Sept 1986
Finished most games ahead: 27½ Pittsburgh 1902
Shortest game: 51 mins NY-Phila 1919
Longest game: 7hrs 23mins SF-NY 1964
Most innings to a game: 26 Brooklyn-Boston 1920
Most runs scored by a team: 28 St Louis v. Phila 1929
Most consecutive victories: 26 New York 1916 (1 tie)
Highest game attendance: 78,672 LA-SF 1958
Highest home season attendance: 3,608,881 LA 1982

NL PLAYER GAME RECORDS
Most at bats: 11 (by 6 players)
Most runs: 6 Melott 1934, 1944, Frank Torre 1957
Most hits: 7 Rennie Stennett, Pitts 1975
Most RBIs: 12 James Bottomley, St Louis 1924
Most home runs: 4 (by 6 players)
Most stolen bases: 5 (by 5 players)

NL PLAYER SEASON RECORDS
Highest batting average: 424 Rogers Hornsby, St Louis 1924
At bats: 701 Juan Samuel, Phila 1984
Runs: 158 Charlie Klein, Phila 1930
Hits: 254 F. O'Doul 1929, W. Terry 1930
RBIs: 190 Lewis Wilson, Chicago 1930
Home runs: 56 Lewis Wilson, Chic 1930
Stolen bases: 118 Lou Brock, St Louis 1974
Wins by a RH pitcher: 37 Christy Mathewson, NY 1908
Wins by a LH pitcher: 27 S. Koufax 1966, S. Carlton 1972
Most losses: 29 Vic Willis, Boston 1905
Lowest ERA: 1.12 Bob Gibson, St Louis 1968
Strikeouts: 382 Sandy Koufax, LA 1965
Most games saved: 45 Bruce Sutter, St Louis 1984
Most innings pitched: 434 Joe McGinnity, NY 1903

NL PLAYER CAREER RECORDS
Most games in NL: 3,562 Pete Rose 1963 to date.
At bats: 14,053 Pete Rose
Runs: 2,165 Pete Rose
Hits: 4,256 Pete Rose
RBIs: 2,202 Hank Aaron
Home runs: 733 Hank Aaron (755 in all)
Stolen bases: 938 Lou Brock
Youngest player: 15yrs 10m 11 days Joe Nuxhall, Cinc 1944
Oldest player: 52yrs 29 days James O'Rourke, NY 1904
Most seasons as player: 24 Pete Rose (still playing)
Most years as manager: 32 John McGraw
Most years as umpire: 27 Bill Klem

Darryl Strawberry, leading batter with the 1986 Mets but unhappy at the club in 1987.

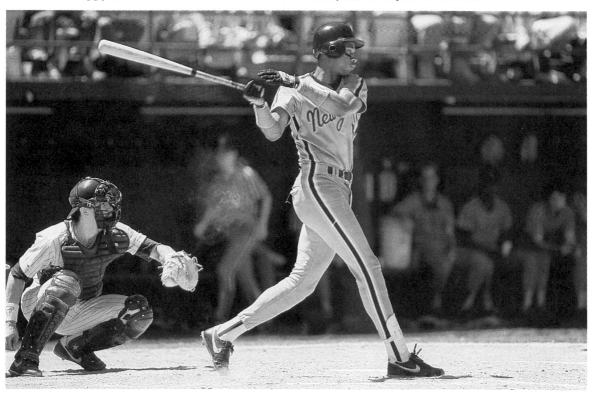

BASEBALL WRITERS' ASSOCIATION MVP AWARDS (so called since 1931)

National League Winners
See p. 125 for an explanation of the abbreviations, which denote playing position.

Year	Player	Club
1911	Frank Schulte	Chicago, of
1912	Lawrence Doyle	New York, 2b
1913	Jacob Daubert	Brooklyn, 1b
1914	John Evers	Boston, 2b
1924	Arthur Vance	Brooklyn, p
1925	Rogers Hornsby	St Louis, 2b
1926	Robert O'Farrell	St Louis, c
1927	Paul Waner	Pittsburgh, of
1928	James Bottomley	St Louis, 1b
1929	Rogers Hornsby	Chicago, 2b
1931	Frank Frisch	St Louis, 2b
1932	Charles Klein	Philadelphia, of
1933	Carl Hubbell	New York, p
1934	Dizzy Dean	St Louis, p
1935	Gabby Hartnett	Chicago, c
1936	Carl Hubbell	New York, p
1937	Joe Medwick	St Louis, of
1938	Ernie Lombardi	Cincinnati, c
1939	Bucky Walters	Cincinnati, p
1940	Frank McCormick	Cincinnati, 1b
1941	Dolph Camilli	Brooklyn, 1b
1942	Mort Cooper	St Louis, p
1943	Stan Musial	St Louis, of
1944	Marty Marion	St Louis, ss
1945	Phil Cavarretta	Chicago, 1b
1946	Stan Musial	St Louis, 1b
1947	Bob Elliott	Boston, 3b
1948	Stan Musial	St Louis, of
1949	Jackie Robinson	Brooklyn, 2b
1950	Jim Konstanty	Philadelphia, p
1951	Roy Campanella	Brooklyn, c
1952	Hank Sauer	Chicago, of
1953	Roy Campanella	Brooklyn, c
1954	Willie Mays	New York, of
1955	Roy Campanella	Brooklyn, c
1956	Don Newcombe	Brooklyn, p
1957	Henry Aaron	Milwaukee, of
1958	Ernie Banks	Chicago, ss
1959	Ernie Banks	Chicago, ss
1960	Dick Groat	Pittsburgh, ss
1961	Frank Robinson	Cincinnati, of
1962	Maury Wills	Los Angeles, ss
1963	Sandy Koufax	Los Angeles, p
1964	Ken Boyer	St Louis, 3b
1965	Willie Mays	San Francisco, of
1966	Roberto Clemente	Pittsburgh, of
1967	Orlando Cepeda	St Louis, 1b
1968	Bob Gibson	St Louis, p
1969	Willie McCovey	San Francisco, 1b
1970	Johnny Bench	Cincinnati, c
1971	Joe Torre	St Louis, 3b
1972	Johnny Bench	Cincinnati, c
1973	Pete Rose	Cincinnati, of
1974	Steve Garvey	Los Angeles, 1b

Ryne Sandberg, NL MVP 1984, when he batted .314 with 200 hits and 114 runs.

Year	Player	Club
1975	Joe Morgan	Cincinnati, 2b
1976	Joe Morgan	Cincinnati, 2b
1977	George Foster	Cincinnati, of
1978	Dave Parker	Pittsburgh, of
1979	Willie Stargell	Pittsburgh, 1b
	Keith Hernandez	St Louis, 1b
1980	Mike Schmidt	Philadelphia, 3b
1981	Mike Schmidt	Philadelphia, 3b
1982	Dale Murphy	Atlanta, of
1983	Dale Murphy	Atlanta, of
1984	Ryne Sandberg	Chicago, 2b
1985	Willie McGee	St Louis, of
1986	Mike Schmidt	Philadelphia, 3b
1987		

Fernando Valenzuela, Mexican pitcher who was NL MVP, Cy Young Award winner and Rookie of the Year in 1981.

CY YOUNG MEMORIAL AWARD

Pitcher of the Year in the National League

Year	Pitcher	Club
1956	Donald Newcombe	Brooklyn
1957	Warren Spahn	Milwaukee
1960	Vernon Law	Pittsburgh
1962	Don Drysdale	Los Angeles
1963	Sandy Koufax	Los Angeles
1965	Sandy Koufax	Los Angeles
1966	Sandy Koufax	Los Angeles
1967	Mike McCormick	San Francisco
1968	Bob Gibson	St Louis
1969	Tom Seaver	New York
1970	Bob Gibson	St Louis
1971	Ferguson Jenkins	Chicago
1972	Steve Carlton	Philadelphia
1973	Tom Seaver	New York
1974	Mike Marshall	Los Angeles
1975	Tom Seaver	New York
1976	Randy Jones	San Diego
1977	Steve Carlton	Philadelphia
1978	Gaylord Perry	San Diego
1979	Bruce Sutter	Chicago
1980	Steve Carlton	Philadelphia
1981	Fernando Valenzuela	Los Angeles
1982	Steve Carlton	Philadelphia
1983	John Denny	Philadelphia
1984	Rick Sutcliffe	Chicago
1985	Dwight Gooden	New York
1986	Mike Scott	Houston
1987		

THE AMERICAN LEAGUE

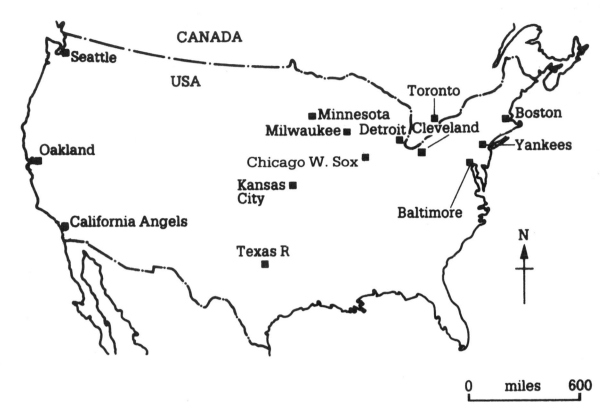

The American League was organised in 1900, twenty-four years after the National League. For this reason it is called the 'junior circuit' by National League fans. The tag does not imply any inferiority in playing ability; American League clubs won forty-eight of the first eighty-three World Series.

The American League has fourteen franchises, divided into an East Division and a West Division.

West Division
California Angels
Chicago White Sox
Kansas City Royals
Minnesota Twins
Oakland Athletics
Seattle Mariners
Texas Rangers

East Division
Baltimore Orioles
Boston Red Sox
Cleveland Indians
Detroit Tigers
Milwaukee Brewers
New York Yankees
Toronto Blue Jays

Each club plays a regular season of 162 games but as there are two more teams than in the National League, the fixture structure is different. Each club plays the seven teams in the other division twelve times, six games at home and six away. Each club also plays the other six teams in

its own division thirteen times. Three of the clubs are played six games at home and seven games away, while the other three are played seven games at home and six away. As each American League club plays eighty-four games against teams in its division and seventy-eight games against the others, they cannot do well by just concentrating on beating teams from the same division.

Of the 1,134 regular season games played in 1987, 70 per cent were at night but only 28 per cent were played on artificial turf.

At the end of the regular season the winners of each division playoff in the best of seven games, ALCS (American League Championships Series), for the league pennant. The champion club then plays the National League champion in the annual best of seven games, World Series. In 1987 the American League champion has the advantage of hosting the first and second games, before the playoff moves to the National League stadium for games 3, 4, and, if needed, game 5. If a sixth or seventh game is necessary, they will be played back in the American League ballpark.

Club name: BALTIMORE ORIOLES
League/Division: American, East
Postal address: Memorial Stadium, Baltimore, Maryland 21218, USA
History of franchise: Milwaukee Brewers 1901, St Louis Browns 1902–53, Baltimore Orioles since 1954
Won East Div. (since 1969): 1969, 70, 71, 73, 74, 79, 83
Won AL (since 1954): 1966, 69, 70, 71, 79, 83
Won World Series (since 1954): 1966, 1970, 1983
Position in div. 1982 to 1986: 2nd, 1st, 5th, 4th, 7th
1987 spring training site: Miami Stadium, Miami, Florida
1987 Minor League farm club teams: AAA – Rochester; AA – Charlotte; A – Hagerstown, Newark; Rookie – Bluefield

First baseman Eddie Murray was 1977 AL Rookie of the Year and AL All-Star 1981 to 1985.

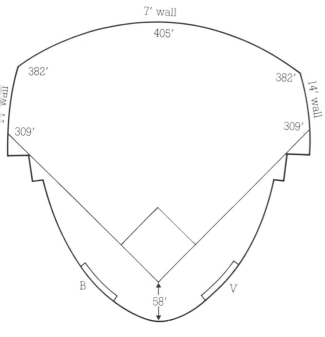

7' wall
405'
382'   382'
14' wall
309'   309'
B   V
58'

FACTS ABOUT MEMORIAL STADIUM
Location: 33rd Street, Ellerslie Ave., 36th Street &
Ednor Road
Capacity: 54,002
Playing surface: grass
1987 day games: 16 (+24 away)
      night games: 65 (+57 away)
1987 ticket prices: $2.50 to $9.50
Radio: WCBM 680 AM
TV/cable: WMAR (2)/Home Team Sports

Ballpark details
Memorial Stadium was built on a thirty-acre plot
in the north of Baltimore owned by the city
authorities, at a cost of $6m. The site had been
occupied by the old Municipal Stadium, used by
the Orioles of the International League, and the
Baltimore Colts of the NFL. The American League
Orioles moved in from St Louis in April 1954, with
the first game being preceded by a massive
parade through the city.

    Memorial Stadium soon gained a reputation as
one of the better 'traditional' ballparks around the
league, having a fine atmosphere and knowledgeable fans. Many were sad, not least the many
squirrels who lived in it, when the old hand-
operated scoreboard was demolished in 1970 to
make way for a larger electric version.

BALTIMORE ORIOLES in 1987

Manager: Cal Ripken Snr, 1st yr with Orioles, 1st yr in majors as manager.

Orioles in '86: W-73 L-89 .451 finished 22½ behind Boston.

AL rankings: batting 8th, pitching 10th.

Rookie manager Cal Ripken Snr can cling to one crumb of comfort this season, things can only get better – 1986 was the worst in Orioles history. In early August the team had been only 2½ games out of first place, but then lost forty-two of their last fifty-six games to finish last. Baltimore's main weaknesses are the starting pitching (so long a strength of the club), their poor fielding, and lack of speed. This season, the infield and longball hitting has been strengthened by Ray Knight from the Mets, but the starting pitchers, and base running outfield still look indifferent.

Pitching: Starting pitchers Mike Boddicker, Mike Flanagan, and Scott McGregor have each won twenty games in a season, but those days seem long gone. Tom Niedenfuer, Jeff Ballard and rookie Eric Bell make up the numbers in a rotation that muddles through as best it can until relievers Mark Williamson, Ken Dixon and ace set-up man Dave Schmidt, and closer Don Aase can rescue the situation.

Catcher: Underrated Terry Kennedy does his best for his pitchers.

Infielders: Eddie Murray and Rick Burleson recovered from poor starts to the season, but All-Star Cal Ripken Jnr, Alan Wiggins and Ray Knight (who seemed to have broken the World Series MVP jinx by leading the AL in batting, until his head injury against Kansas City) have played consistently well, with Rick Barleson in the platoon.

Outfielders: John Shelby, Fred Lynn, and rookie Ken Gerhart look under pressure from reserves/designated hitters, Larry Sheets, Lee Lacy, Mike Young and Jim Dwyer.

Left: Consistent catcher, Terry Kennedy. NL All-Star 1981 and 1985.

Below: Pitcher Dave Schmidt has had the best season of his seven-year ML career.

Club name: BOSTON RED SOX
League/Division: American, East
Postal address: Fenway Park, 4 Yawkey Way,
Boston, Massachusetts 02215,
USA
History of franchise: Boston Red Sox formed
1901
Won East Div. (since 1969): 1975, 1986
Won AL: 1903, 04, 12, 15, 16, 18, 46, 67, 75, 86
Won World Series: 1903, 12, 15, 16, 18
Position in div. 1982 to 1986: 3rd, 6th, 4th, 5th,
1st
1987 spring training site: Chain O'Lakes,
Winter Haven, Florida
1987 Minor League farm club teams: AAA –
Pawtucket; AA – New Britain; A – Greensboro,
Winter Haven, Elmira

*Left: Consistent third
baseman Wade Boggs
– a superb career
batting average of .350
in six seasons
with Boston.*

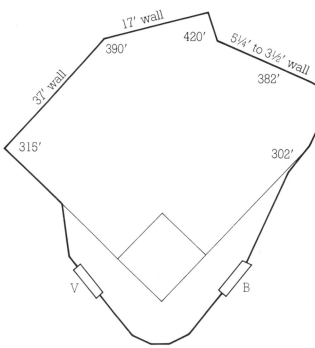

Above: Outfielder Dwight Evans has played over 2,000 games for Boston in 16 season.

FACTS ABOUT FENWAY PARK
Location: Yawkey Way, Lansdowne Street, and Ipswich Street
Capacity: 33,583
Playing surface: grass
1987 day games: 31 (+24 away)
     night games: 50 (+57 away)
1987 ticket prices: $5 to $14
Radio: WPLM 1390 AM, WRKO 680 AM
TV/cable: WSBK (38)/New England Sports

Ballpark details
Fenway Park was named after 'The Fens', a marshy area near Ipswich Street, and opened in April 1912 at the time that the *Titanic* sank. One of the oldest and most loved of Major League ballparks, its obstructions and eccentric dimensions would not be approved if the stadium were being built today.

Fenway Park is dominated by the 37ft high wall beyond left field. (The 23ft high wire mesh screen was added in 1936 to protect the houses across the street.) For many years the wall was a gaudy advertising board but it was painted green in 1947 and is now known as the 'Green Monster'. Whatever its colour, the wall has continued to lure some right-handed hitters into unwisely changing their batting style by attempting to pull the ball across them towards the short boundary in left field.

In 1945, the appropriately named Philadelphia outfielder, Hal Peck, hit a piegon in flight with a throw which was deflected to second base where the base runner was tagged out.

The hand-operated scoreboard has two white strips of dots and dashes that spell out in Morse code the initials of Tom and Jean Yawkey, the late Red Sox owner and his widow.

With high-topped shoes to protect his weak ankles, first baseman Bill Buckner has played over 2,200 games in 19 seasons with the Dodgers, Cubs and Boston since 1984. NL All-Star 1981.

BOSTON RED SOX in 1987

Manager: John McNamara, 3rd yr with Red Sox, 15th yr in majors, W-927 L-952.

Red Sox in '86: W-95 L-66 .590 won East division by 5½ games.

AL rankings: batting 2nd, pitching 3rd.

If last winter was not bad enough after losing the World Series, spring training was worse. The front office made little effort in the close season to improve the club's relief pitching, speed on the bases, or its fielding. They did not even bother to resign free agent, catcher and team catalyst Rich Gedman, which kept him out of the lineout until May. With little strength in depth, the team may regret relying on the same starting pitchers and powerful but static batters having another great season.

Pitching: Ace starter Roger Clemens held out for twenty-nine days in a dispute over his new two-year contract, which was settled at $1.8m plus incentives. Al Nipper, Bob Stanley, Jeff Sellers, John Leister and Bruce Hurst made an indifferent start, but mercurial Dennis Boyd's neck and shoulder injuries affected the balance of the rotation, which does well not to rely too much on set-up relievers Joe Sambito and Steve Crawford, or closers Calvin Schiraldi and Wes Gardner.

Catcher: Marc Sullivan filled in for Rich Gedman.

Infielders: Bill Buckner's weak ankles and Marty Barrett's wrist are not fully compensated for by the consistently brilliant All-Star Wade Boggs. Spike Owen, Glenn Hoffman, and Ed Romero compete for infield positions.

Outfielders: Injury hit Dwight Evans and Jim Rice are given mixed support by centre fielder Dave Henderson and rookies Ellis Burks and Mike Greenwell.

Designated hitter/reserves: Don Baylor has played well since his transfer from the Yankees.

Club name: CLEVELAND INDIANS
League/Division: American, East
Postal address: Cleveland Stadium, Cleveland, Ohio 44114, USA
History of franchise: Cleveland Indians formed 1901
Yet to win East Div. (since 1969)
Won AL: 1920, 1948, 1954
Won World Series: 1920, 1948
Position in div. 1982 to 1986: 6th, 7th, 6th, 7th, 5th
1987 spring training site: Hi Corbett Field, Tucson, Arizona
1987 Minor League farm club teams: AAA – Buffalo; AA – Waterbury; A – Kinston, Waterloo; Rookie – Burlington

Versatile Joe Carter has played over 400 games for the Indians.

FACTS ABOUT MUNICIPAL STADIUM

Location: Boudreau Boulevard
Capacity: 74,208
Playing surface: grass
1987 day games: 28 (+27 away)
    night games: 53 (+54 away)
1987 ticket prices: $3 to $9
Radio: WWWE 1100 AM
TV: WUAB-TV (43)

Ballpark details

Cavernous Municipal Stadium was built for $3m on a convenient site on the south shore of Lake Erie in only a year. Its first sporting event was a heavyweight boxing match which drew a large crowd, and the first baseball game in July 1932 attracted 76,979 curious spectators. When times got hard, the Indians played at the smaller League Park, but moved to the giant bowl permanently in 1947.

One of baseball's most dramatic moments took place in Cleveland in 1941, when more than 67,000 fans saw the Yankees batter Joe DiMaggio have his hitting streak halted after fifty-six consecutive games.

Despite its vocal, knowledgeable fans, the atmosphere is never what it might be. The stadium is so vast that it seems empty if the crowd is anything less than 30,000.

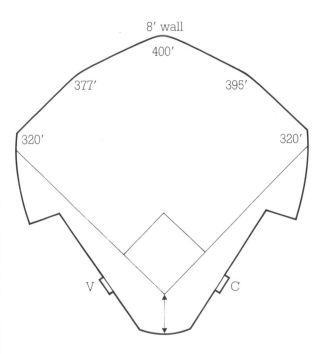

Left: Pitcher Ken Schrom has appeared in over 150 games.
Below: Dominican shortstop Julio Franco.
Right: Second year relief pitcher Scott Bailes appeared in 62 games for Cleveland in 1986.

CLEVELAND INDIANS in 1987

Manager: Pat Corrales, 5th yr with Indians, 9th yr in majors, W-541 L-578.

Indians in '86: W-84 L-78 .519 finished 11½ games behind Boston.

AL rankings: batting 1st, pitching 12th.

Many forecasters thought this was the Year of the Indian, but despite a string of exciting youngsters, club officials thought the team still one year away from contention. Although the batting looks great, the main problem is the weak pitching, not helped by some indifferent fielding.

Pitching: Starters Ken Schrom, Scott Bailes, Greg Swindell, and knuckleball pitchers Tom Candiotti and the senior current major leader, 48-year-old Phil Niekro started listlessly. Relievers Ed Vande Berg, Rich Yett and Mark Huismann were not much better, while all-time great Steve Carlton picked up as a reliever is always good value.

Catcher: Rick Dempsey (from Baltimore) and knuckleball catcher Chris Bando.

Infielders: Joe Carter, Julio Franco, Brook Jacoby and shortstops Cory Snyder and Tony Bernazard.

Outfielders: Cory Snyder sometimes plays in the deep, Brett Butler (injured in early season), and left-hander Mel Hall have potential, but look fragile.

Designated hitter/reserves: Fading Andre Thornton has been replaced by Pat Tabler, with Carmen Castillo in reserve.

Club name: DETROIT TIGERS
League/Division: American, East
Postal address: Tiger Stadium, Detroit,
                    Michigan 48216, USA
History of franchise: Detroit Tigers formed 1901
Won East Div. (since 1969): 1972, 1984
Won AL: 1907, 08, 09, 34, 35, 40, 45, 68, 84
Won World Series: 1935, 45, 68, 84
Position in div. 1982 to 1986: 4th, 2nd, 1st, 3rd, 3rd
1987 spring training site: Marchant Stadium, Lakeland, Florida
1987 Minor League farm club teams: AAA – Toledo; AA – Glens Falls; A – Lakeland, Fayetteville; Rookie – Bristol

1978 NCAA football All-American outfielder Kirk Gibson.

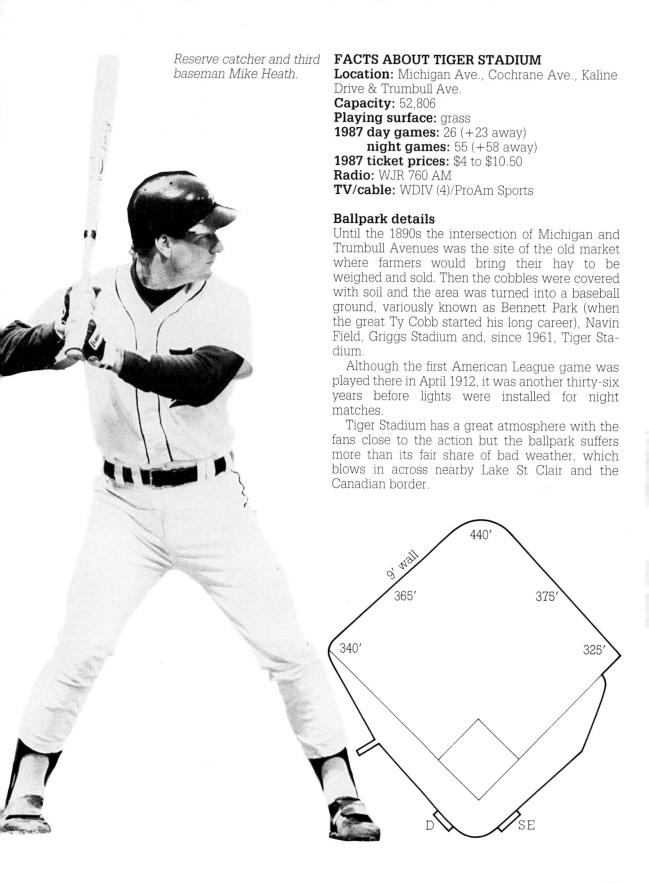

Reserve catcher and third baseman Mike Heath.

FACTS ABOUT TIGER STADIUM
Location: Michigan Ave., Cochrane Ave., Kaline Drive & Trumbull Ave.
Capacity: 52,806
Playing surface: grass
1987 day games: 26 (+23 away)
    night games: 55 (+58 away)
1987 ticket prices: $4 to $10.50
Radio: WJR 760 AM
TV/cable: WDIV (4)/ProAm Sports

Ballpark details
Until the 1890s the intersection of Michigan and Trumbull Avenues was the site of the old market where farmers would bring their hay to be weighed and sold. Then the cobbles were covered with soil and the area was turned into a baseball ground, variously known as Bennett Park (when the great Ty Cobb started his long career), Navin Field, Griggs Stadium and, since 1961, Tiger Stadium.

Although the first American League game was played there in April 1912, it was another thirty-six years before lights were installed for night matches.

Tiger Stadium has a great atmosphere with the fans close to the action but the ballpark suffers more than its fair share of bad weather, which blows in across nearby Lake St Clair and the Canadian border.

440'

9' wall

365'   375'

340'   325'

D   SE

1985 AL All-Star pitcher, Dan Petry, has won over 100 games since his debut with Detroit in 1979.

DETROIT TIGERS in 1987

Manager: Sparky Anderson, 9th yr with Tigers, 18th yr in majors W-1,513 L-1,122.

Tigers in '86: W-87 L-75 .537 finished 8½ games behind Boston.

AL rankings: batting 6th, pitching 6th.

A number of the same players are still at Detroit who helped win the 1984 World Series. They have a shrewd manager, two great pitchers, and are good fielders. However, too many seem past their best, and the team lost its free agent, All-Star catcher Lance Parrish (to Philadelphia). The lack of talent in depth means that the stars must stay healthy if the team is to do well.

Pitching: Unsettled free agent Jack Morris (who has won more games in the past decade than any other pitcher), eventually re-signed for $1.85m and is far and away the club's best pitcher. Fellow starters Frank Tanana, Walt Terrell, Eric King and unsettled Dan Petry try to ensure they hand a close score to star, middle-inning reliever Willie Hernandez (who has had a shoulder injury and tends to give up too many home runs) or Mark Thurmond, rookies Mike Henneman, and Jeff Robinson.

Catcher: Rookie Matt Nokes is rivalled as a batter by Mike Heath, but neither can be compared with Parrish, yet.

Infielders: Veteran Darrell Evans and Dave Bergman, All-Star Lou Whitaker, error prone Darnell Coles, or Tom Brookens and batting shortstop Alan Trammell must be on top form to gather the cheap hits given up by their pitchers.

Outfielders: Kirk Gibson, ailing Chet Lemon, and Pat Sheridan will be pressed for their places by Larry Herndon and Billy Bean.

Designated hitter/reserves: Bill Madlock, Matt Nokes and Johnny Grubb.

66

Club name: MILWAUKEE BREWERS
League/Division: American, East
Postal address: Milwaukee County Stadium,
　　　　　　　　Milwaukee, Wisconsin 53214,
　　　　　　　　USA
History of franchise: Seattle Pilots 1969,
Milwaukee Brewers since 1970
Won East Div. (since 1969): 1982
Won AL: 1982
Yet to win World Series
Position in div. 1982 to 1986: 1st, 5th, 7th, 6th,
6th
1987 spring training site: Compadre Stadium,
Chandler, Arizona
1987 Minor League farm club teams: AAA –
Denver; AA – El Paso; A – Stockton, Beloit; Rookie
– Helena

Above: Rookie catcher B. J. Surhoff.
Below: 30-year-old first baseman Greg Brock.

FACTS ABOUT COUNTY STADIUM
Location: 46th Street, off Bluemound Road
Capacity: 53,192
Playing surface: grass
1987 day games: 31 (+20 away)
    night games: 50 (+61 away)
1987 ticket prices: $3.50 to $10
Radio: WTMJ 620 AM
TV/cable: WVTV (18)

Ballpark details
In 1950, County Stadium was built for $5m near Lake Michigan for the Boston Braves Minor League farm club, which played in the American Association. Only three years later, the Boston club, which had been losing money heavily in New England, moved in and became the Milwaukee Braves. At first the team drew six times as many fans as they had in Boston, but all too soon gates declined and the Braves moved on to Atlanta, leaving County Stadium unused by Major League baseball except for twenty games played in the late 1960s by the White Sox.

In 1970, the bankrupt Seattle Pilots moved to Milwaukee and became the Brewers. Despite the heroics of the free-hitting Brewers of 1982, the franchise is probably best known for its tailgate parties in the car parks, and superb 'Brewer Food'.

MILWAUKEE BREWERS in 1987
Manager: Tom Trebelhorn, 1st yr with Brewers, 1st yr in majors.
Brewers in '86: W-77 L-84 .478 finished 18 games behind Boston.
AL rankings: batting 9th, pitching 5th.

Milwaukee's improbable rookie manager, ex-school teacher Tom Trebelhorn (appointed to oversee the implementation of the Brewer youth programme), was always going to be a catalytic hero or a sad joke. But even he cannot have expected the underrated Brewers to win their first thirteen games in 1987 (equalling Atlanta's record, set in 1982). Soon afterwards they lost 12 in a row, so many expected the Brewers to run out of gas by September, particularly as the Yankees stayed within a couple of games, but the players had already done more than anyone could have expected of them, besides adding romance and interest (twenty-four TV crews and 125 reporters watched the winning streak ended by Chicago), to the 1987 season.

When the streak reached twelve in a row, Webb Restaurants in Milwaukee honoured a promise made by the chain's founder, the late George Webb, in 1953, and on one day gave away about 100,000 hamburgers in their forty-eight fast food restaurants.

Pitching: Ace starter Teddy Higuera leads a promising rotation of Bill Wegman, Paul Mirabella, Lex Baker, Juan Nieves, rookie Mike Birkbeck who are supported by top reliever Dan Plesac, Mark Clear and rookie Chris Bosio.

Catcher: Rookie B. J. Surhoff holds off Bill Schroeder, with young Ramser Correa signed for the future.

Infielders: Greg Brock, hometown boy Jim Gantner, Paul Molitor and shortstop Dale Sveum did well until lynchpin Molitor was injured, but Castillo filled in.

Outfielders: Rob Deer, perennial Brewers favourite Robin Yount, and Glenn Braggs started well, but the strong hitting disguised some suspect fielding and a lack of speed.

Designated hitter/reserves: Veteran Cecil Cooper's place has been under threat from the youngsters such as Paciorek, O'Brien, Manning and Robidoux, who are getting playing time in Trebelhorn's platoon system. A few may be traded away in order to improve the pitching rotation.

Right: 32-year-old outfielder, Robin Yount, has played most of his 1,900 games for the Brewers at shortstop.

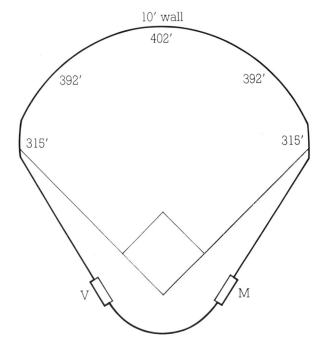

10' wall
402'
392'   392'
315'   315'
V   M

Club name: NEW YORK YANKEES
League/Division: American, East
Postal address: Yankee Stadium, Bronx, New York 10451, USA
History of franchise: Baltimore Orioles 1901–2, New York Yankees since 1903
Won East Div. (since 1969): 1976, 77, 78, 81
Won AL: 1921, 22, 23, 26, 27, 28, 32, 36, 37, 38, 39, 41, 42, 43, 47, 49, 50, 51, 52, 53, 55, 56, 57, 58, 60, 61, 62, 63, 64, 76, 77, 78, 81
Won World Series: 1923, 27, 28, 32, 36, 37, 38, 39, 41, 43, 47, 49, 50, 51, 52, 53, 56, 58, 61, 62, 77, 78
Position in div. 1982 to 1986: 5th, 3rd, 3rd, 2nd, 2nd
1987 spring training site: Fort Lauderdale Stadium, Fort Lauderdale, Florida
1987 Minor League farm club teams: AAA – Columbus; AA – Albany – Colonie; A – Fort Lauderdale, Prince William, Oneonta; Rookie – Sarasota

FACTS ABOUT YANKEE STADIUM
Location: East 161st Street & River Ave.
Capacity: 57,545
Playing surface: grass
1987 day games: 24 (+25 away)
night games: 57 (+56 away)
1987 ticket prices: $3 to $10
Radio: WABC 770 AM
TV/cable: WPIX (11)/Sports Channel

Ballpark details
From the day that Babe Ruth hit the first home run at Yankee Stadium in April 1923, more has been written about it than any other ballpark.

The Yankees originally played in Manhattan, at Hilltop Park and the Polo Grounds, but in 1922 building started on a twelve-acre site in The Bronx beside the Harlem River, where baseball had been played back in the 1860s.

Although the Yankees kept collected title after title, the stadium was starting to look as rundown as the neighbourhood. So for two years in the early 1970s the team moved in with their cross-town rivals, the Mets, while the old stadium was remodelled for about $60m. Today, the historic atmosphere and monuments beyond centrefield remain, but the district did not give its name to the 'Bronx Cheer' for nothing.

Right: Pitcher Charles Hudson.
Far right: Pitcher Tommy John has appeared in 700 games in the majors.
Inset: Hitter Don Mattingly.

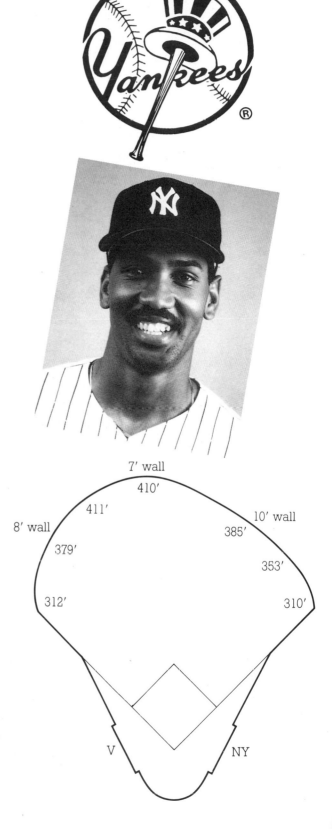

NEW YORK YANKEES in 1987

Manager: Lou Piniella, 2nd yr with Yankees, 2nd yr in majors, W-90 L-72.

Yankees in '86: W-90 L72 .556 finished 5½ games behind Boston.

AL rankings: batting 2nd, pitching 9th.

Owner George Steinbrenner did not say much when the Yankees' cross-town rivals, the Mets, won the World Series. He knew that his team (particularly the starting pitchers and the farm system) did not compare favourably with the set-up over in Queens, so he traded a few players in the off-season to improve the team's fielding, made a stir by not signing two great free agent pitchers, Jack Morris and the Yankees own, Ron Guidry, and worked towards recovering the big title, the baseball championship of New York. Everything started pretty well, so Steinbrenner remained quiet, but the old, loud George will surely reappear when the pennant is on the line.

Pitching: Starters Dennis Rasmussen, revitalised Charles Hudson, Tommy John (44), and Rick Rhoden from Pittsburgh see the game through to Dave Righetti, who set the Major League record of 46 saves in 1986, or Pat Clements, Tom Stoddard, Bob Tewksbury, and Cecilio Guante. Free agent Ron Guidry resigned in May.

Catcher: Joel Skinner and Rick Cerone were joined by Mark Salas.

Infielders: Perennial All-Star Don Mattingly (no doubt inhibited by his $1,975,000 salary), Willie Randolph and Mike Pagliarulo got off to slow starts, but shortstop Wayne Tolleson and the deep fielders more than made up for that.

Outfielders: Gary Ward has helped both base stealer extraordinary Rickey Henderson, and his fellow All-Star Dave Winfield.

Designated hitter/reserves: Mark Easter, Claudell Washington, Dan Pasqua, Ron Kittle and Lenn Sakata.

Yankees skipper, second baseman Willie Randolph has played in over 1,500 games since being traded from Pittsburgh in 1975. AL All-Star 1977, 1980 and 1981.

Club name: TORONTO BLUE JAYS
League/Division: American, East
Postal address: Box 7777, Adelaide St Post Office, Toronto, Ontario M5C 2K7, Canada
History of franchise: Toronto Blue Jays formed 1977
Won East Div. (since 1969): 1985
Yet to win AL or World Series
Position in div. 1982 to 1986: 6th, 4th, 2nd, 1st, 4th
1987 spring training site: Grant Field, Dunedin, Florida
1987 Minor League farm club teams: AAA – Syracuse; AA – Knoxville; A – Dunedin, Myrtle Beach, St Catherines; Rookie – Medicine Hat

Rookie pitcher Jeff Musselman graduated with a BA in economics from Harvard University in 1985.

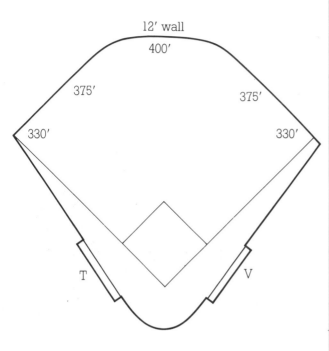

12' wall
400'
375'   375'
330'   330'

T   V

FACTS ABOUT EXHIBITION STADIUM
Location: Exhibition Place via Lakeshore Blvd
Capacity: 43,737
Playing surface: artificial turf
1987 day games: 34 (+24 away)
       night games: 47 (+57 away)
1987 ticket prices: $4 to $14
Radio: CJCL 1430 AM
TV/cable: CFTO (99)/Sports Network

Ballpark details
Exhibition Stadium was built in the mid-1970s for
Canadian $18m in a 350-acre fairground park
beside Lake Ontario in central Toronto. The first
Major League baseball game was played there in
April 1977, when over 44,000 fans shivered
through the snow flurries as the Blue Jays beat the
White Sox. The stands have an unusual layout,
which prevents spectators getting as close to the
action as they might elsewhere. This is because
the massive Astroturf playing surface is used by
the Argonauts of the CFL.

The Blue Jays' loyal supporters will be rewarded
in 1989 when the club moves indoors to the
Canadian $240m domed stadium (which will have
a retractable roof 280ft above the playing field)
being built at the foot of the C. N. Tower in central
Toronto.

*Above: 1986 AL All-Star outfielder Jesse Barfield
hit 40 home runs for Toronto in 1986.*

*Right: Pitcher John Cerutti was selected in the first
round of the 1981 free agent draft, but has only
recently fulfilled his potential.*

TORONTO BLUE JAYS in 1987

Manager: Jimy Williams, 2nd yr with Blue Jays, 2nd yr in majors, W-86 L-76.

Blue Jays in '86: W-86 L-76 .537 finished 9½ games behind Boston.

AL rankings: batting 4th, pitching 7th.

Manager Jimy Williams knows the Blue Jays look good on paper. They have powerful hitters and speedy fielders. The team also has one of the best outfields in the majors, but there is something about the club (perhaps its Canadian location) that keeps them being regarded as outsiders. Maybe all that will change when the team moves indoors, to The Dome, in 1989. For the present, the starting pitching seems fragile and there is a lack of depth to the roster.

Pitching: Jimmy Key, Jeff Musselman, Jose Nunez, Jim Clancy, Joe Johnson, John Cerutti and slow recovering Dave Stieb will be needed for about six innings before set-up reliever Mark Eichhorn and closer Tom Henke finish the game.

Catcher: Ernie Whitt does a competent job for his pitchers but he needs help.

Infielders: Willie Upshaw, rookie Mike Sharperson, Kelly Gruber, and base stealing shortstop Tony Fernandez are overshadowed by the outfielders.

Outfielders: George Bell, unsettled base stealer Lloyd Moseby, and Jessie Barfield will need to repeat their heroics of 1986 if Toronto is to fulfil its potential.

Designated hitter/reserves: Rance Mulliniks, Rick Leach, rookie Fred McGriff, Cecil Fielder and Garth Iorg.

Club name: CALIFORNIA ANGELS
League/Division: American, West
Postal address: PO Box 2000, Anaheim,
California 92803, USA
History of franchise: California Angels formed
1961 (called Los Angeles Angels 1961–65)
Won West Div. (since 1969): 1979, 1982, 1986
Yet to win AL or World Series
Position in div. 1982 to 1986: 1st, 5th, 2nd, 2nd,
1st
1987 spring training site: Mesa, Arizona
Home games at Angels Stadium, Palm Springs,
California
1987 Minor League farm club teams: AAA –
Edmonton; AA – Midland; A – Palm Springs,
Davenport, Salem

Far left: Shortstop Dick Schofield.
Left: Catcher/outfielder, turned designated hitter,
Brian Downing.
Above: Anaheim Stadium.

FACTS ABOUT ANAHEIM STADIUM
Location: 2000 State College Boulevard
Capacity: 64,573
Playing surface: grass
1987 day games: 24 (+26 away)
     night games: 57 (+55 away)
1987 ticket prices: $3 to $8
Radio: KMPC 710AM, XPRS (Spanish) 1090AM
TV: KTLA (5)

Ballpark details
The Angels spent their first few seasons sharing
Dodger Stadium until their own $24m ballpark at
Anaheim was ready. The ground-breaking cere-
mony on the 140-acre site with the Santa Ana
Mountains in the background had been attended
by a number of stars from nearby Disneyland.
Judging by the time it took for the stadium to be
ready, it seemed that some of the cartoon charac-
ters must have been involved in the construction
work. The first game was not played until April
1966, and even that had comic overtones, as
flooding (from a broken water main) delayed the
start by twenty minutes.

Anaheim's most conspicuous landmark from
the three freeways near the ground is the 230ft-
high letter 'A' that now stands in the car park
beyond right field.

For all its teething troubles, the baseball fans of
southern California are lucky indeed, as dual-use
Anaheim is arguably the only ballpark that rivals
Dodger Stadium.

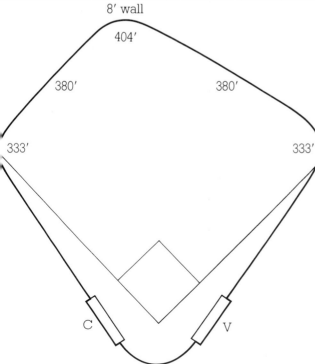

8' wall
404'
380'   380'
333'   333'
C   V

CALIFORNIA ANGELS in 1987

Manager: Gene Mauch, 5th yr with Angels, 26th yr in majors, W-1,828 L-1,950.

Angels in '86: W-92 L-70 .568 won West division by 5 games.

AL rankings: batting 9th, pitching 2nd.

California must be the sentimental favourites this season, after Gene Mauch's team was just one strike away from the World Series for the first time in 1986.

The loss of Reggie Jackson and Bobby Grich may not prove as telling as early season problems for pitchers Candelaria and McCaskill, and being without free agent catcher Bob Boone until May.

The youngsters have plenty of opportunities to contribute with the bat this season and must do so if the club is to beat the Royals for another chance at the pennant in October.

Pitching: Starters Mike Witt, veteran Don Sutton, John Candelaria, Kirk McCaskill and Jerry Reuss, hand over to relievers Willie Fraser, rookie Gary Lucas, set-up man Chuck Finley and closers Donnie Moore and De Wayne Buice.

Catcher: Butch Wynegar and Darrell Miller stood in for Bob Boone with Jack Fimple.

Infielders: Last year's hot-starter and All-Star Wally Joyner, basestealing rookie Mark McLemore, veteran Doug DeCinces and shortstop Dick Schofield are a fine unit, joined by rookie Gus Polidor.

Outfielders: Speedy Jamaican rookie Devon White, Gary Pettis and young Jack Howell are as mobile an outfield as one could wish to see, pressed by Ruppert Jones.

Designated hitter/reserves: Veteran Brian Downing, rookie Mark Ryal and George Hendrick .

Third baseman Doug DeCinces.

Club name: CHICAGO WHITE SOX
League/Division: American, West
Postal address: Comiskey Park, 324 W. 35th Street, Chicago, Illinois 60616, USA
History of franchise: Chicago White Sox formed 1901
Won West Div. (since 1969): 1983
Won AL: 1901, 06, 17, 19, 59
Won World Series: 1906, 1917
Position in div. 1982 to 1986: 3rd, 1st, 5th, 3rd, 5th
1987 spring training site: Payne Park, Sarasota, Florida
1987 Minor League farm club teams: AAA – Hawaii; AA – Birmingham; A – Peninsula, Daytona Beach; Rookie – Sarasota

Venezuelan shortstop Ozzie Guillen was 1985 AL Rookie of the Year.

FACTS ABOUT COMISKEY PARK
Location: Dan Ryan at 35th Street
Capacity: 44,087
Playing surface: grass
1987 day games: 19 (+25 away)
   night games: 62 (+56 away)
1987 ticket prices: $4 to $10.50
Radio: WMAQ 670 AM
TV/cable: WFLD (32)/Sportsvision

Ballpark details
When Charles A. Comiskey brought his club to Chicago he leased Southside Park, home of the Chicago Cricket Club, until able to build the team's present home, Comiskey Park. In those days, south Chicago had a large Irish community, so to keep in with the locals, Comiskey made sure that the foundation stone was green.

The first American League game was played in July 1910, which makes it the oldest Major League ballpark still in use. Comiskey made sure that the stadium was always being modernised and improved, which explains why it is in good condition. It has all the baseball atmosphere one would expect of such an historic ballpark, including Bill Veeck's first exploding scoreboard. However, it suffers from the same weather hazards that affect all the lakeside stadiums.

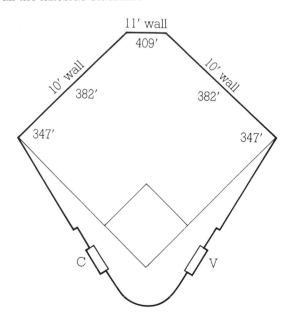

Infielder Tim Hulett.

CHICAGO WHITE SOX in 1987

Manager: Jim Fregosi, 1st full season with White Sox, 6th yr in majors, W-282 L-299.

White Sox in '86: W-72 L-90 .444 finished 20 games behind Angels.

AL rankings: batting 14th, pitching 3rd.

It will be interesting to see how many fans go to Comiskey Park to watch a White Sox team built on solid pitching and error free fielding, rather than spectacular hitting in the American League tradition. If attendances are down, the fact will be seized on by those who wish to move the club to Chicago's outer suburbs.

New manager Jim Fregosi has been successful at California and must establish a positive attitude if the players are to fulfil their potential. The pitching looks strong but the batting is weak enough without having Carlton Fisk unhappy because they will not let him play as catcher every day.

Pitching: The starters Floyd Bannister, Joel Davis, Jose DeLeon, Rich Dotson and Neil Allen put too much work on relievers Ray Searage, rookie Joel McKeon, Bob Thigpen, Bob James, and Jim Winn.

Catcher: Ron Hassey and rookie Ron Karkovice may keep Carlton Fisk in the dugout.

Infielders: Greg Walker, Carlos Manrique, Donnie Hill, and Tim Hulett try hard but cannot look good alongside star shortstop Ozzie Guillen.

Outfielders: Ivan Calderon, base stealer Gary Redus and Harold Baines look good with Daryl Boston and Kenny Williams in the platoon.

Designated hitter/reserves: Veteran Carlton Fisk, Ron Hassey and Jerry Royster.

Below: The infield tarpaulin protects Comiskey Park from a squall off Lake Michigan.
Right: Outfielder Harold Baines was the first player selected in the June 1977 free agent draft. AL All-Star 1985 and 1986.

Bo Jackson may yet play
NFL football for the
Raiders in 1988 if he can
get his contract changed.

Club name: KANSAS CITY ROYALS

League/Division: American, West
Postal address: PO Box 419969, Kansas City,
Missouri 64141, USA
History of franchise: Kansas City Royals formed
1969
Won West Div. (since 1969): 1976, 77, 78, 80, 84,
85
Won AL: 1980, 1985
Won World Series: 1985
Position in div. 1982 to 1986: 2nd, 2nd, 1st, 1st,
3rd
1987 spring training site: Terry Park, Fort
Myers, Florida
1987 Minor League farm club teams: AAA –
Omaha; AA – Memphis; A – Fort Myers,
Appleton, Eugene; Rookie – Sarasota

FACTS ABOUT ROYALS STADIUM

Location: Harry S. Truman Sports Complex, One
Royal Way
Capacity: 40,625
Playing surface: artificial turf
1987 day games: 16 (+26 away)
    night games: 65 (+55 away)
1987 ticket prices: $3 to $10
Radio: WIBW 580AM, KMBZ 980AM
TV: WDAF (4)

Ballpark details

In the 1920s, there was a frog pond and ash tip at
the corner of 22nd Street and Brooklyn, but today
the site is occupied by the $70m Harry S. Truman
Sports Complex with Arrowhead Stadium.

The first Kansas City Major League franchise
was moved to Oakland by owner Charles O. Finley
when he became fed up with waiting for a new
ballpark to be built. When the 1969 expansion
team was formed, it also played at Municipal
Stadium but moved to attractive, neat, Royals
Stadium (the first to have Astroturf in the American League) in April 1973. The ballpark is certainly one of the best in the majors and features an
unusual attraction. Beyond the centrefield fence
there is a 'water fountain spectacular' in which
the height of the water responds to the volume of
cheering.

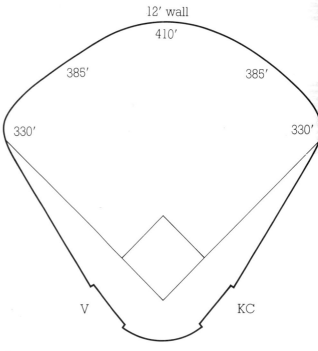

*Pitcher Bret Saberhagen won 20 games in 1985.
Wearing No. 18 (not 31) in this his comeback year.*

KANSAS CITY ROYALS in 1987

Manager: Billy Gardner, 1st yr with Royals, 6th yr in majors, W-268 L-353.

Royals in '86: W-76 L-86 .469 finished 16 games behind Angels.

AL rankings: batting 12th, pitching 1st.

If Kansas City's two star pitchers have fully recovered from their injuries, and Dick Howser's traumas galvanise rather than distract the club, then the Royals could win the division. Dick Howser was the popular manager who guided the team to the 1985 World Series, but after winning the 1986 All-Star Game as the AL manager, had to go into hospital for a number of operations on a brain tumor. He died on 17 June.

Most of the players remain from the World Series team, while Bo Jackson and Danny Tartabull add hitting power to the line up. The club kept winning when Brett was injured – a sure sign of success.

Jackson (from Auburn University), won NCAA football's Heisman Trophy in 1985, and is one of the few good runners on the team. After a few weeks in 1986 with the Royals AA farm club, the Memphis Chicks, he was called up to the Major League roster. A few football fans are still amazed that Jackson turned his back on the NFL (the Buccaneers and Raiders have tried to sign him this year), but Bo does not regret his decision.

Pitching: Starters Bret Saberhagen, Charlie Leibrandt are classy, Dave Gumpert, Danny Jackson and Mark Gubicza need support from Jerry Gleaton, Steve Farr, Bud Black, and ace reliever Dan Quisenberry, who must return to his 1985 form if the club is to beat the Angels. Saberhagen bounced back so well thanks to shoulder exercises that all the Royals pitchers now follow.

Catcher: Jamie Quirk, Larry Owen and Ed Hearn (injured shoulder) help the pitchers and bat well.

Infielders: Steve Baboni, Frank White and All-Star George Brett are experienced but all have injury doubts. Weak hitting shortstop Angel Salazar is reliable.

Outfielders: Speedy rookie Bo Jackson and experienced Willie Wilson have their work cut out keeping the ball away from fielding liability Danny Tartabull. Rookie sensation Kevin Seitzer helps spread the workload at third base on in the deep.

Designated hitter/reserves: Batting coach Hal McRae, Juan Beniquez, Jorge Orta and Thad Bosley.

Pitcher Charlie Leibrandt has won over 40 games in his last 3 seasons.

Club name: MINNESOTA TWINS
League/Division: American, West
Postal address: HHH Metrodome, 501 Chicago Ave South, Minneapolis, Minnesota 55415, USA
History of franchise: (1st) Washington Senators 1901–60, Minnesota Twins since 1961
Won West Div. (since 1969): 1969, 1970
Won AL (since 1961): 1965
Yet to win World Series since 1961
Position in div. 1982 to 1986: 7th, 5th, 2nd, 4th, 6th
1987 spring training site: Tinker Field, Orlando, Florida
1987 Minor League farm club teams: AAA – Portland; AA – Orlando; A – Visalia, Kenosha; Rookie – Elizabethton

Relief pitcher Jeff Reardon was a most valuable trade from the Expos.

FACTS ABOUT HUBERT H. HUMPHREY METRODOME

Location: 501 Chicago Avenue South
Capacity: 55,244
Playing surface: artificial turf and roof
1987 day games: 23 (+24 away)
     night games: 58 (+57 away)
1987 ticket prices: $3 to $9
Radio: WCCO 830AM
TV: KMSP (9)

Ballpark details

In the late 1970s there was real concern in the twin cities that the Twins and the NFL Vikings would leave the area. However, the sale of bonds and the old ballpark raised about $80m which was used to build the Hubert H. Humphrey Metrodome, on a twelve-acre plot in east central Minneapolis near the Mississippi River. Remarkably for modern construction projects, the spartan dome was built $2m under budget, and the first Major League game was played in it in April 1982.

The stadium has a 186ft high roof, made of a translucent fibreglass fabric supported by steel cables; twenty air fans ensure any snow melts and drains quickly away. The blowers also help keep the stadium at 70°F while the twin cities shiver.

The original Astroturf carpet was replaced in 1987 at a cost of $1.5m.

Above left: Kirby Puckett.
Below left: Pitcher Mark Portugal.
Right: Versatile Randy Bush.

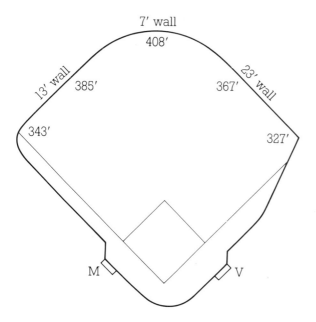

MINNESOTA TWINS in 1987

Manager: Tom Kelly, 1st full yr with Twins, 1st full yr in majors, W-12 L-11.
Twins in '86: W-71 L-91 .438 finished 21 games behind Angels.
AL rankings: batting 7th, pitching 14th.

Minnesota's rookie manager Tom Kelly knows that with Kirby Puckett fit, his team can score plenty of runs. His problem in the off-season was to improve the pitching and the lackadaisical attitude of the club. Opponents seem to steal bases at will. Apart from the shrewd move of obtaining Jeff Reardon from Montreal, the club also replaced its Astroturf with a new, less bouncy carpet in the hope that it might help the home team's pitchers. However, the carpet will not help to reduce the many homers conceded.

Pitching: Starters Mike Smithson, Keith Atherton, Frank Viola, Joe Niekro, Dan Schatzeder, Mark Portugal and Les Straker have simple instructions – survive long enough for ace relievers Dutch born Bert Blyleven, Juan Berenguer, George Frazier, and Jeff Reardon (The Terminator) to finish the game.

Catcher: Tom Nieto and Tim Laudner compete.

Infielders: Kent Hrbek, Steve Lombardozzi, Al Newman and Greg Gagne cannot out-hit nor outfield third baseman Gary Gaetti.

Outfielders: Dan Gladden, All-Star Kirby Puckett, and Tom Brunansky look good, but the line up is unsettled.

Designated hitter/reserves: Veteran Roy Smalley, Randy Bush, and rookie Gene Larkin.

Club name: OAKLAND ATHLETICS
League/Division: American, West
Postal address: Oakland-Alameda County
Coliseum, Oakland,
California 94621, USA
History of franchise: Philadelphia Athletics
1901–54, Kansas City Athletics 1955–67, Oakland
As/Athletics since 1968
Won West Div. (since 1969): 1971, 72, 73, 74, 75,
81
Won AL (since 1968): 1972, 1973, 1974
Won World Series (since 1968): 1972, 1973, 1974
Position in div. 1982 to 1986: 5th, 4th, 4th, 4th,
4th
1987 spring training site: Pheonix Municipal
Stadium, Pheonix, Arizona
1987 Minor League farm club teams: AAA –
Tacoma; AA – Huntsville; A – Modesta, Madison,
Medford

FACTS ABOUT OAKLAND-ALAMEDA COUNTY COLISEUM

Location: Nimitz Freeway & Hegenberger Road
Capacity: 48,219
Playing surface: grass
1987 day games: 41 (+19 away)
    night games: 40 (+62 away)
1987 ticket prices: $3 to $9
Radio: KSFO 560 AM
TV: KPIX (5)

Ballpark details

Work started on the Oakland-Alameda County Coliseum in the south of Oakland beside Nimitz Freeway on the east of San Francisco Bay in April 1964. The first American League game played there, four years later, was attended by ex-baseball broadcaster and then Governor of California Ronald Reagan, who threw out the first ball.

Although the ballpark has much to recommend it, not least the sound system which is used for the odd bursts of rock music. However, fans are further from the action than at most grounds.

The woeful financial plight of the Oakland franchise a couple of years ago helped bring about the current era of fiscal responsibility in the majors.

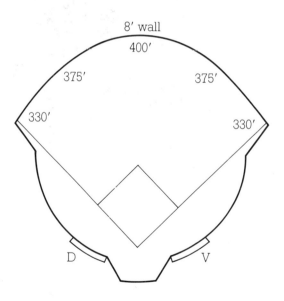

Left: Cuban, Jose Canseco, 1986 AL Rookie of Year.

Above right: Catcher Mickey Tettleton.

Right: Pitcher Gene Nelson, traded from the White Sox.

OAKLAND ATHLETICS in 1987

Manager: Tony LaRussa, 1st full yr with Athletics, 9th yr in majors, W-567 L-544.
As in '86: W-76 L-86 .469 finished 16 games behind Angels.
AL rankings: batting 13th, pitching 11th.

The franchise has reverted to its original name, the prodigal son Reggie Jackson has returned home, Jose Canseco gets better every day, and manager Tony LeRussa had a good record when he took over the club for the second half of last season. However, these are not good enough reasons to think that this Oakland team can win the World Series. The starting pitchers and the outfielding is still suspect.

Pitching: Starters Moose Haas, Joaquin Andujar and Dave Stewart, who seem recovered from injury, are joined by Curt Young and Steve Ontiveros, before relievers Gene Nelson, Dennis Eckersley and Jay Howell take over to finish the game.

Catcher: Rookie Terry Steinbach bats better than Mickey Tettleton.

Infielders: Injury hit Carney Lansford, but Tony Phillips, rookie home run slugger Mark McGwire and shortstop Alfredo Griffin are a solid-looking unit, supported by Mike Callego.

Outfielders: Young star Jose Canseco, Golden Glove Dwayne Murphy, and Mike Davis look good when fit, and have Stan Javier and Luis Polonia in reserve.

Designated hitter/reserves: Veterans Reggie Jackson (now past 550 home runs in his career), and Ron Cey.

Right: Oakland born Dave Stewart had pitched for LA, Texas and Philadelphia before coming home.

Far right: First base man, Alvin Davis, 1984 AL Rookie of Year.

Club name: SEATTLE MARINERS
League/Division: American, West
Postal address: PO Box 4100, 411 First Ave,
Suite 480, Seattle, Washington
98104, USA
History of franchise: Seattle Mariners formed
1977
Yet to win West Div., AL, or World Series
Position in div. 1982 to 1986: 4th, 7th, 5th, 6th,
7th
1987 spring training site: Tempe Diablo
Stadium, Tempe, Arizona
1987 Minor League farm club teams: AAA –
Calgary; AA – Chattanooga; A – Salinas, Wausau,
Bellingham

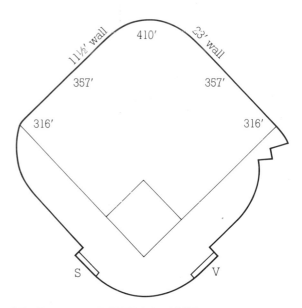

FACTS ABOUT THE KINGDOME
Location: 201 South King Street
Capacity: 59,438
Playing surface: artificial turf and roof
1987 day games: 21 (+26 away)
    night games: 60 (+55 away)
1987 ticket prices: $3 to $9
Radio: KIRO 710 AM
TV: KIRO (7), KTZZ (22)

Ballpark details
The original Seattle Major League franchise, the Pilots, played in Sick's Stadium, but when the club left for Milwaukee, plans were made for a new ballpark.

In 1972, a plot on the south side of Seattle's city centre was earmarked for the $67m domed dual-use stadium, which would have a roof 250ft above the Astroturf playing field. The first Major League game in the Kingdome was played in April 1977, and although it was soon clear that the ball carried better than in the original Astrodome, it shared the slightly dull atmosphere for baseball found in other roofed stadiums. Although the fans are able to watch the games in comfort the dome deprives them of the stunning view of Puget Sound and the Cascade Mountains.

Right: Pitcher Mike Trujillo traded from Boston.

Inset: Third baseman Jim Presley takes pre-game batting practice.

Below: Seattle manager, Dick Williams (58).

SEATTLE MARINERS in 1987
Manager: Dick Williams, 1st full yr with Mariners, 20th yr in majors, W-1,468 L-1,334.
Mariners in '86: W-67 L-95 .414 finished 25 games behind Angels.
AL rankings: batting 11th, pitching 13th.

Seattle is a franchise in the middle of a storm. About the only consistent feature in recent years is that it keeps on losing (games, money, and spectators). Owner George Argyros seems more interested in the San Diego Padres.

Last season the Mariners failed to make the most of the good conditions for hitters in the Kingdome, then traded away the best slugger they had, Danny Tartabull. Fortunately, the fielding and the pitching, have improved, while Phil Bradley, Moses, and Reynolds are 'running fools' on the base paths. Dick Williams may surprise those people who bother to watch.
Pitching: Starters Scott Bankhead, star left-hander Mark Langston, Bill Wilkinson, Jerry Reed, Lee Guetterman and the three Mikes – Moore, Trujillo, and Morgan, are backed by star relievers Steve Shields and Edwin Nunez.
Catcher: Free-hitting Scott Bradley has competition from rookie David Valle, and Bob Kearney.
Infielders: Unsettled Alvin Davis, Harold Reynolds, Jim Presley and shortstop Rey Quinones have John Moses in a promising platoon.
Outfielders: All-Star Phil Bradley had a dreadful start with the bat, so was little help to rookie Mickey Brantley, Mike Kingery and John Christensen.
Designated hitter/reserves: Ken Phelps has become the major home run threat since Tartabull has left.

Club name: TEXAS RANGERS

League/Division: American, West

Postal address: PO Box 1111, Arlington, Texas 76010, USA

History of franchise: (2nd) Washington Senators 1961–71, Texas Rangers since 1972
Yet to win West Div., AL or World Series since 1972

Position in div. 1982 to 1986: 6th, 3rd, 7th, 7th, 2nd

1987 spring training site: Rangers Stadium, Port Charlotte, Florida

1987 Minor League farm club teams: AAA – Oklahoma City; AA – Tulsa; A – Port Charlotte, Gastonia; Rookie – Sarasota

FACTS ABOUT ARLINGTON STADIUM

Location: 1500 Copeland Road

Capacity: 43,508

Playing surface: grass

1987 day games: 8 (+28 away)
　　　night games: 73 (+53 away)

1987 ticket prices: $2.25 to $9

Radio: WBAP 820 AM

TV: KTVT (11)

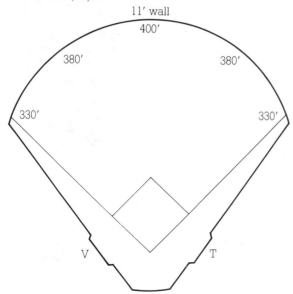

Above: Puerto Rican, Ruben Sierra.

Left: Infielder Scott Fletcher has played over 600 games in seven years.

Ballpark details

Turnpike Stadium was built in the mid-1960s for the Dallas-Fort Worth Spurs of the AA Texas League. Then, when the second Washington Senators franchise moved to Texas in 1972, it was gradually expanded and improved.

Situated at Arlington on Route 30, midway between Dallas and Fort Worth, Arlington Stadium takes advantage of the dual catchment area and visitors drawn by the nearby 'Six Flags over Texas' amusement park. The first capacity crowd turned out in June 1973 to witness the fairy tale Major League debut of eighteen-year-old David Clyde, signed from a Houston high school, who pitched five innings to win his first ever game.

Although the stadium has a good reputation, the strength-sapping Texas heat means that only about eight home games a season are played during daylight.

TEXAS RANGERS in 1987
Manager: Bobby Valentine, 2nd yr with Rangers, 2nd yr in majors, W-140 L-151.
Rangers in '86: W-87 L-75 .537 finished 5 games behind Angels.
AL rankings: batting 5th, pitching 8th.

Manager Bobby Valentine did extremely well last season to forge a good young, but experienced squad and establish a winning attitude. To maintain the belief and momentum the team needed a good start this season with the young pitching staff winning games through their good control, and the support of their fielders.

Below: Rookie Malloy, was given Mason's number when called up this year.
Right: Bruce Hurst, a Boston star in 1986.

Pitching: The rotation has potential with starters injury prone Bobby Witt, Edwin Correa, rookie Mike Loynd, Jose Guzman, and knuckleball thrower Charlie Hough. Relievers Mitch Williams and Dale Mohorcic are joined by Greg Harris who can pitch right- or left-handed. He may need to.
Catcher: Don Slaught may edge Darrell Porter, rookie Mike Stanley and Gino Petralli behind the plate.
Infielders: Pete O'Brien, rookie Jerry Browne, and Steve Buechele are light hitters compared with shortstop Scott Fletcher.
Outfielders: Pete Incaviglia, Oddibe McDowell, rookie Bob Brower and Ruben Sierra must contribute with the bat all season if the Rangers are to stay with the Royals.
Designated hitter/reserves: Larry Parrish, veteran Tom Paciorek, and Curtis Wilkerson.

AMERICAN LEAGUE PENNANT WINNERS

Year	Club	W.	L.	Pct.	G.A.	Year	Club	W.	L.	Pct.	G.A.
1901	Chicago	83	53	.610	4	1961	New York	109	53	.673	8
1902	Philadelphia	83	53	.610	5	1962	New York	96	66	.593	5
1903	Boston	91	47	.659	14½	1963	New York	104	57	.646	10½
1904	Boston	95	59	.617	1½	1964	New York	99	63	.611	1
1905	Philadelphia	92	56	.622	2	1965	Minnesota	102	60	.630	7
1906	Chicago	93	58	.616	3	1966	Baltimore	97	63	.606	9
1907	Detroit	92	58	.613	1½	1967	Boston	92	70	.568	1
1908	Detroit	90	63	.588	½	1968	Detroit	103	59	.636	12
1909	Detroit	98	54	.645	3½	1969	Baltimore (E)	109	53	.673	19
1910	Philadelphia	102	48	.680	14½	1970	Baltimore (E)	108	54	.667	15
1911	Philadelphia	101	50	.669	13½	1971	Baltimore (E)	101	57	.639	12
1912	Boston	105	47	.691	14	1972	Oakland (W)	93	62	.600	5½
1913	Philadelphia	96	57	.627	6½	1973	Oakland (W)	94	68	.580	6
1914	Philadelphia	99	53	.651	8½	1974	Oakland (W)	90	72	.556	5
1915	Boston	101	50	.669	2½	1975	Boston (E)	95	65	.594	4½
1916	Boston	91	63	.591	2	1976	New York (E)	97	62	.610	10½
1917	Chicago	100	54	.649	9	1977	New York (E)	100	62	.617	2½
1918	Boston	75	51	.595	2½	1978	b) New York (E)	100	63	.613	1
1919	Chicago	88	52	.629	3½	1979	Baltimore (E)	102	57	.642	8
1920	Cleveland	98	56	.636	2	1980	Kansas City (W)	97	65	.599	14
1921	New York	98	55	.641	4½	1981	c) New York (E)	59	48	.551	–
1922	New York	94	60	.610	1	1982	Milwaukee (E)	95	67	.586	1
1923	New York	98	54	.645	16	1983	Baltimore (E)	98	64	.605	6
1924	Washington	92	62	.597	2	1984	Detroit (E)	104	58	.642	15
1925	Washington	96	55	.636	8½	1985	Kansas City (W)	91	71	.562	1
1926	New York	91	63	.591	3	1986	Boston (E)	95	66	.590	5½
1927	New York	110	44	.714	19	1987					
1928	New York	101	53	.656	2½						
1929	Philadelphia	104	46	.693	18						
1930	Philadelphia	102	52	.662	8						
1931	Philadelphia	107	45	.704	13½						
1932	New York	107	47	.695	13						
1933	Washington	99	53	.651	7						
1934	Detroit	101	53	.656	7						
1935	Detroit	93	58	.616	3						
1936	New York	102	51	.667	19½						
1937	New York	102	52	.662	13						
1938	New York	99	53	.651	9½						
1939	New York	106	45	.702	17						
1940	Detroit	90	64	.584	1						
1941	New York	101	53	.656	17						
1942	New York	103	51	.669	9						
1943	New York	98	56	.636	13½						
1944	St Louis	89	65	.578	1						
1945	Detroit	88	65	.575	1½						
1946	Boston	104	50	.675	12						
1947	New York	97	57	.630	12						
1948	a) Cleveland	97	58	.626	1						
1949	New York	97	57	.630	1						
1950	New York	98	56	.636	3						
1951	New York	98	56	.636	5						
1952	New York	95	59	.617	2						
1953	New York	99	52	.656	8½						
1954	Cleveland	111	43	.721	8						
1955	New York	96	58	.623	3						
1956	New York	97	57	.630	9						
1957	New York	98	56	.636	8						
1958	New York	92	62	.597	10						
1959	Chicago	94	60	.610	5						
1960	New York	97	57	.630	8						

G.A.: Games ahead of second-place club. a) Defeated Boston in one-game playoff. b) Defeated Boston in one-game playoff to win division. c) First half 34-22; second 25-26 of strike-hit season.

AMERICAN LEAGUE REGULAR SEASON RECORDS SINCE 1900

AL PLAYER SEASON RECORDS

Highest batting average: .422 Napoleon Lajoie, Phila 1901
At bats: 705 Willie Wilson, KC 1980
Runs: 177 Babe Ruth, NY 1921
Hits: 257 George Sisler, St Louis 1920
RBIs: 184 Lou Gehrig, NY 1931
Home runs: 61 Roger Maris, NY 1961
Stolen bases: 130 Rickey Henderson, Oak 1982
Wins by a RH pitcher: 41 John Chesbro, NY 1904
Wins by a LH pitcher: 31 Robert Grove, Phila 1931
Most losses: 26 J. Townsend, Wash 1904; R. Groom, Wash 1909
Lowest ERA: 1.14 Walter Johnson, Wash 1913
Strikeouts: 383 Nolan Ryan, Cal 1973
Most games saved: 46 Dave Righetti, NY 1986
Most innings pitched: 464 Ed Walsh, Chic 1908

AL PLAYER CAREER RECORDS

Most games in AL: 3,308 Carl Yastrzemski 1961–83
At bats: 11,988 Carl Yastrzemski
Runs: 2,245 Ty Cobb
Hits: 4,191 Ty Cobb
RBIs: 2,192 Babe Ruth
Home runs: 708 Babe Ruth (714 in all)
Stolen bases: 892 Ty Cobb
Youngest player: 16 yrs 8m 5 days Carl Scheib, Phila 1943
Oldest player: 59yrs 2m 18 days Leroy Paige, KC 1965
Most seasons as player: 25 Eddie Collins 1906–30
Most years as manager: 50 Connie Mack (53 in all)
Most years as umpire: 31 Tom Connolly

AL TEAM RECORDS

Most wins: 111 Cleveland 1954
Most defeats: 117 Philadelphia 1916
Earliest West Division win: 15 Sept 1971
Earliest East Division win: 13 Sept 1969
Finished most games ahead: 20 Chicago 1983
Shortest game: 55 mins St Louis-New York 1926
Longest game: 8hrs 6 mins Chicago-Milwaukee 1984
Most innings to a game: 25 Chicago-Milwaukee 1984
Most runs scored by a team: 29 Boston v. St Louis 1950
Most consecutive victories: 19 Chicago 1906
Highest game attendance: 84,587 Cleve-NY 1954 doubleheader
Highest home season attendance: 2,807,360 California 1982

AL PLAYER GAME RECORDS

Most at bats: 11 (by 8 players)
Most runs: 6 John Pesky 1946, Spike Owen 1986
Most hits: 9 John Burnett, Cleve 1932
Most RBIs: 11 Tony Lazzeri, NY 1936
Most home runs: 4 Lou Gehrig 1932, Pat Seerey 1948, Rocco Colavito 1959
Most stolen bases: 6 Eddie Collins, Phila twice in 1912

CY YOUNG MEMORIAL AWARD

PITCHER OF THE YEAR IN THE AMERICAN LEAGUE

Year	Pitcher	Club
1958	Bob Turley	New York
1959	Early Wynn	Chicago
1961	Whitey Ford	New York
1964	Dean Chance	Los Angeles
1967	Jim Lonborg	Boston
1968	Dennis McLain	Detroit
1969	Dennis McLain	Detroit
	Mike Cuellar	Baltimore
1970	Jim Perry	Minnesota
1971	Vida Blue	Oakland
1972	Gaylord Perry	Cleveland
1973	Jim Palmer	Baltimore
1974	Jim Hunter	Oakland
1975	Jim Palmer	Baltimore
1976	Jim Palmer	Baltimore
1977	Sparky Lyle	New York
1978	Ron Guidry	New York
1979	Mike Flanagan	Baltimore
1980	Steve Stone	Baltimore
1981	Rollie Fingers	Milwaukee
1982	Pete Vuckovich	Milwaukee
1983	LaMarr Hoyt	Chicago
1984	Willie Hernandez	Detroit
1985	Bret Saberhagen	Kansas City
1986	Roger Clemens	Boston
1987		

Right: Boston pitcher, Roger Clemens, 1986 All-Star, AL MVP, and Cy Young Award winner.

Right inset: The legendary, George 'Babe' Ruth, who played over 2,500 games for Boston Red Sox 1914–19, NY Yankees 1920–34, Boston Braves 1935. He hit 714 home runs, had a career batting average of .342, pitched in 163 games and won 92 of them.

BASEBALL WRITER'S ASSOCIATION MVP AWARDS (so called since 1931)

American League winners
See p. 125 for an explanation of the abbreviations, which denote playing position.

Year	Player	Club
1911	Ty Cobb	Detroit, of
1912	Tris Speaker	Boston, of
1913	Walter Johnson	Washington, p
1914	Eddie Collins	Philadelphia, 2b
1922	George Sisler	St Louis, 1b
1923	Babe Ruth	New York, of

Robin Yount, 1982 AL MVP, and AL All-Star 1980, 1982 and 1983.

1924	Walter Johnson	Washington, p
1925	Roger Peckinpaugh	Washington, ss
1926	George Burns	Cleveland, 1b
1927	Lou Gehrig	New York, 1b
1928	Mickey Cochrane	Philadelphia, c
1931	Lefty Grove	Philadelphia, p
1932	Jimmie Foxx	Philadelphia, 1b
1933	Jimmie Foxx	Philadelphia, 1b
1934	Mickey Cochrane	Detroit, c
1935	Hank Greenberg	Detroit, 1b
1936	Lou Gehrig	New York, 1b
1937	Charles Gehringer	Detroit, 2b
1938	Jimmie Foxx	Boston, 1b
1939	Joe DiMaggio	New York, of
1940	Hank Greenberg	Detroit, of
1941	Joe DiMaggio	New York, of
1942	Joe Gordon	New York, 2b
1943	Spud Chandler	New York, p
1944	Hal Newhouser	Detroit, p
1945	Hal Newhouser	Detroit, p
1946	Ted Williams	Boston, of
1947	Joe DiMaggio	New York, of
1948	Lou Boudreau	Cleveland, ss
1949	Ted Williams	Boston, of
1950	Phil Rizzuto	New York, ss
1951	Yogi Berra	New York, c
1952	Bobby Shantz	Philadelphia, p
1953	Al Rosen	Cleveland, 3b
1954	Yogi Berra	New York, c
1955	Yogi Berra	New York, c
1956	Mickey Mantle	New York, of
1957	Mickey Mantle	New York, of
1958	Jack Jensen	Boston, of
1959	Nelson Fox	Chicago, 2b
1960	Roger Maris	New York, of
1961	Roger Maris	New York, of
1962	Mickey Mantle	New York, of
1963	Elston Howard	New York, c
1964	Brooks Robinson	Baltimore, 3b
1965	Zoilo Versalles	Minnesota, ss
1966	Frank Robinson	Baltimore, of
1967	Carl Yastrzemski	Boston, of
1968	Dennis McLain	Detroit, p
1969	Harmon Killebrew	Minnesota, 1-3b
1970	John (Boog) Powell	Baltimore, 1b
1971	Vida Blue	Oakland, p
1972	Dick Allen	Chicago, 1b
1973	Reggie Jackson	Oakland, of
1974	Jeff Burroughs	Texas, of
1975	Fred Lynn	Boston, of
1976	Thurman Munson	New York, c
1977	Rod Carew	Minnesota, 1b
1978	Jim Rice	Boston, of
1979	Don Baylor	California, of
1980	George Brett	Kansas City, 3b
1981	Rollie Fingers	Milwaukee, p
1982	Robin Yount	Milwaukee, ss
1983	Cal Ripken	Baltimore, ss
1984	Willie Hernandez	Detroit, p
1985	Don Mattingly	New York, 1b
1986	Roger Clemens	Boston, p
1987		

BASEBALL'S HALL OF FAME

In 1934, the President of the National League, Ford C. Frick, asked Major League owners for $100,000 as an initial payment towards setting up a Hall of Fame for baseball at Cooperstown, in east central New York State, 200 miles north of New York City.

This small town of only 2,300 inhabitants was chosen because it was where Abner Graves claimed, in a letter submitted to the Mills Commission of 1905–07, that about sixty years before, in 1839, his schoolfriend, Abner Doubleday, had changed the rules of 'Town Ball' to baseball.

Organised Baseball took the approaching centenary of that occasion and the discovery in 1934 of an old soft baseball in a trunk owned by Graves, only three miles from Cooperstown, to speed the building of a National Baseball Museum in which to display baseball memorabilia, and to create a Hall of Fame to honour the game's greatest figures.

Over the years the buildings have been extended and changed several times in order to display the ever-increasing number of photographs, cuttings, programmes, tickets, paintings, models, uniforms and playing equipment donated to the museum and library by baseball fans from all over the world. The records, audio tapes, and continuous screenings of the multi-award-winning TV show *This Week in Baseball* have helped about 250,000 visitors a year relive many great moments from baseball's exciting past.

On Hall of Fame Day, in late July or early August each year, the newly elected members of the Hall of Fame are inducted by the Commissioner of Baseball in ceremonies held on the steps of the library. The following day, two Major League teams (Braves v. Yankees in 1987) play an exhibition game in front of 10,000 fans at nearby Doubleday Field. (The Doubleday family's strong links with baseball are maintained by Abner's great-nephew, Nelson Doubleday, co-owner of the New York Mets.)

Those elected to the Hall of Fame on 26 July 1987 included Billy Williams and Jim 'Catfish' Hunter. There seems little doubt that, once qualified for election, the following modern Major League stars will one day be given baseball's highest honour.

Hall of Fame exhibits.

Wade Boggs, Boston Red Sox (AL)
Uniform: No. 26 **Position:** Third base
Bats left handed but throws right handed
Born: 15 June 1958 at Omaha, Nebraska
Height: 6ft 2ins, **Weight:** 13st 8lbs
Wade Anthony Boggs was selected by the Red
Sox in the seventh round of the 1976 free agent
draft. After six years in the minors he was brought
up to the Major League roster for the 1982 season.

In his first year, Wade hit .349, an AL record
batting average for a rookie who played in over
100 games. In 1985, he hit a record 187 singles and
was voted an AL All-Star for the first time, an
honour he repeated in 1986.

Never one of baseball's flashy players, Wade has
quietly built career statistics that speak for them-
selves. In some 700 games during his first five
seasons, he accumulated more than 500 runs,
1,000 hits, a remarkable career batting average of
.352 (never falling below .325), and regularly bat-
tles with Don Mattingly of the Yankees for the AL
batting title.

Boggs played in the 1986 ALCS and World
Series but was the first to admit he did not play
well in his first playoffs.

One of Wade's superstitions to help ward off a
batting slump is to eat chicken every day. When it
seemed to work for Wade he wrote a short book of
recipes appropriately entitled *Foul Tips*.

Reggie Jackson, Oakland Athletics (AL)
Uniform: No. 44 **Position:** Designated hitter or outfielder
Bats and throws left-handed.
Born: 18 May 1946 in Wyncote, Pennsylvania
Height: 6ft **Weight:** 14st 12lbs

Reginald Martinez Jackson was selected by the Kansas City As in the June 1966 free agent draft. He made his Major League debut the following season and remained with the franchise for eight years when it moved to Oakland. He played in Baltimore for a year, then went on to further glory with the New York Yankees until 1982, when he returned west to the California Angels. Reggie rejoined the Athletics for 1987.

During his twenty glorious years in the majors, Jackson has played in more than 2,700 games, scored over 1,500 runs, 2,500 hits, 550 home runs (sixth on the all-time list), played in 11 ALCS, and 5 World Series, 12 All-Star Games, and was voted the American League's MVP in 1973.

As one of the most recognised sportsmen in America, Reggie has profited from numerous advertising contracts, and works enthusiastically on behalf of a variety of charities, including one concerned with Amyothropic Lateral Sclerosis (often called Lou Gehrig disease, after the great Yankees slugger).

Pete Rose, Cincinnati Reds (NL)
Uniform: No. 14 **Position:** First base or pinch hitter
Bats right or left handed, and throws right hand
Born: 14 April 1941 at Cincinnati, Ohio
Height: 5ft 11ins, **Weight:** 14st 7lbs
Peter Edward Rose was signed as a free agent by the Reds in 1960. After three seasons in the minor, his spectacular debut as a second baseman and outfielder led to him being voted Rookie of the Year in 1963.

In 1979, Pete signed for Philadelphia, then played half a season for Montreal before being traded back home to Cincinnati as player-manager in August 1984.

By the end of the 1986 regular season, Pete 'Charley Hustle' Rose had established by his heads-up, no nonsense style, a host of major league and NL career records (most games 3,562, most hits 4,256, most at-bats 14,053, and most seasons 24, to name but a few).

Rose has played in seven NLCS, six World Series, sixteen All-Star games for the NL, was voted the National League's MVP in 1973, and the Player of the Decade 1970–79.

In his first two full years as the Reds' manager Rose lifted the club from fifth to second in the NL West. A pointer to the club's future might be indicated by this year's swarm of chirping cicadas. The last plague in Cincinnati was in 1970 the first year of the Reds' five NL pennants in seven seasons.

Although Pete left himself off the playing roster for the early months of 1987, he may well be tempted to add to his records if the Reds make the playoffs.

Gary Carter, New York Mets (NL)

Uniform: No. 8 **Position:** Catcher
Throws and bats right-handed.
Born: 8 April 1954 in Culver City, California
Height: 6ft 2ins **Weight:** 15st

Gary Edmund Carter was acquired by the Montreal Expos in the June 1972 free agent draft and signed straight from high school. He spent five seasons in the Minor Leagues before being called up to the Expos roster in 1974. He started as an outfielder but took over as catcher in 1977. After eleven years in Montreal he was traded to the Mets in exchange for four good players.

Despite surgery to his knees, a suspect arm and other injuries during the past thirteen seasons, Carter has played in almost 1,700 games, hit over 270 home runs, and had 1,000 RBIs, a career batting average of .271, and won three Golden Gloves for his fielding. However, his contribution to the team cannot be expressed simply in terms of statistics.

Gary has played in eight All-Star Games, two NLCS (for Montreal and the Mets) and played a major role in the New York club's World Series victory in 1986.

Away from the ballpark, he is heavily involved each year in a number of charity events, particularly those on behalf of the Leukemia Society.

George Brett, Kansas City Royals (AL)
Uniform: No. 5 **Position:** Third base
Bats left-handed, throws right-handed.
Born: 15 May 1953 in Glendale, West Virginia
Height: 6ft **Weight:** 14st

George Howard Brett was selected by Kansas City in the June 1971 free agent draft, he then spent three years in the Minor Leagues before making his Major League debut in 1973.

During the past thirteen seasons George has missed more than 200 games because of a variety of injuries, yet played in more than 1,700 fixtures, scored over 1,000 runs, 2,000 hits, 200 home runs and has the excellent career batting average of .314. Only Hall-of-Famers Ty Cobb and Lou Gehrig have won more AL batting divisions.

In 1981, Brett averaged .390 (the closest to the magic .400 since 1941) and was voted American League MVP of the year.

George has been selected for eleven consecutive All-Star Games since 1976, played in six ALCS (averaging .340), and two World Series (averaging .373). He recently signed a five-year contract which brought him $2.08m in 1987. Together with his two younger brothers and elder brother Ken (a former Major League pitcher), the boys own the Spokane Padres of the North West (Class A) League.

Fernando Valenzuela, Los Angeles Dodgers (NL)
Uniform: No. 34 **Position:** Pitcher
Pitches and throws left-handed.
Born: 1 November 1960 at Navajoa, Sonora, Mexico
Height: 5ft 11ins **Weight:** 14st 4lbs

Fernando Anguamea Valenzuela was purchased by the Dodgers from Puebla of the Mexican League (Class AAA) in July 1979, and almost immediately established himself as the best screw ball pitcher in the majors.

In his seven years with the Dodgers, Fernando has pitched over 1,500 innings, won just over 100 games of his 160 appearances, gained about 1,300 strikeouts, and has a career Earned Run Average of only 2.94.

He was voted National League Cy Young Award winner and Rookie of the Year in 1981, has been selected for six All-Star Games, played in three NLCS, and won his only game pitching in the World Series.

Valenzuela is a national hero in Mexico where his games are carried live on radio and television, and an inspiration to the many Mexicans in southern California struggling to make a living in a foreign land. They are proud of how Fernando has succeeded and created a good life for his large family, despite being unable to speak English for some years and coming from a poor family in a rural part of Mexico.

...an Ryan, Houston Astros (NL)
...form: No. 34 **Position:** Pitcher
...ches and bats right-handed.
...rn: 31 January 1947 in Refugio, Texas
...ight: 6ft 2ins **Weight:** 15st

...nn Nolan Ryan was selected by the New York
...ets in the June 1965 free agent draft. The
...lowing season he pitched his way straight from
...ass A Minor League baseball into the majors,
...ut then missed most of the 1967 season because
...f military service. He was back with the Mets in
...968 and saved game 4 of his team's fairy-tale win
...n the 1969 World Series. Ryan was traded to the
...California Angels (AL) in 1972 where he played for
...eight seasons before being signed as a free agent
...by Houston for 1980.

After 250 wins (five were no-hitters) in over 600
appearances during the past twenty years in the
majors, Nolan's consistent success has enabled
him to create records that will take some beating.
Renowned for his extra-fast pitching (officially
timed by the Rockwell Corporation in 1974 at
100.8 mph), he has a total of more than 4,200
strikeouts in 4,000 innings, with a record haul of
382 strikeouts in 1973.

Ryan has been chosen for six All-Star Games
(representing both leagues), played in four NLCS
and one World Series, but has yet to win baseball's
top honour for a pitcher, the annual Cy Young
Award.

THE MAJOR LEAGUE ALL-STAR GAME

From the earliest days of the Major Leagues fans had wondered and argued which players they would select for the best team in baseball. With no serious or regular international competition, this exercise remained a pipe dream until Arch Ward, sports editor of the *Chicago Tribune* newspaper, used Chicago's impending Century of Progress Exposition as the excuse to campaign for a 'Dream Game', a Game of the Century, to be played between the stars of the National and American leagues, selected by balloting the fans, with the game being underwritten by the *Tribune*.

Ward canvassed Commissioner Landis, the two league presidents, and the clubs, and found that only three National League owners were against the idea. Gradually he convinced everyone that the All-Star Game would be good mid-season publicity for baseball battling through the great Depression, and so the first game was played at Comiskey Park, Chicago, on Thursday, 6 July 1933.

Over 47,000 fans attended the game and saw the Americans managed by Connie Mack, wearing their club uniforms, beat the specially uniformed Nationals, managed by John McGraw.

For twelve years up to 1947, All-Star teams were selected by the managers, but for the following ten years the fans chose the players while that year's manager (usually the man who had managed in the previous World Series) selected the pitchers and any others he wanted in the squad of between 18 to 29 players.

In 1956 and 1957, Cincinnati fans swamped the ballot with their votes making sure the club provided at least four starting players, so until 1969 the players, coaches and managers selected the rosters.

Since 1970, fan ballots have been distributed during June at Major League ballparks for the fans to cast their votes. From 1987, the balloting will be sponsored for three seasons by *USA Today* newspaper. Players may be added to the squad and every club must have at least one representative involved.

Ironically, Arch Ward's funeral was on the day of the twenty-second All-Star Game in 1955, but he had lived long enough to see his brainchild become a sporting institution. Today, the three-day All-Star break in mid-July marks the symbolic halfway point in the Major League season, and the sell-out game itself always generates a great deal of interest and spectacular action from the best players in the professional game.

ALL-STAR GAME RESULTS

Year	Site/Date	Winner/Loser
1933	Comiskey Park, Chicago	AL 4, NL 2
1934	Polo Grounds, New York	AL 9, NL 7
1935	Municipal Stadium, Cleveland	AL 4, NL 1
1936	Braves Field, Boston	NL 4, AL 3
1937	Griffith Stadium, Washington	AL 8, NL 3
1938	Crosley Field, Cincinnati	NL 4, AL 1
1939	Yankee Stadium, New York	AL 3, NL 1
1940	Sportsman's Park, St Louis	NL 4, AL 0
1941	Briggs Stadium, Detroit	AL 7, NL 5
1942	Polo Grounds, New York	AL 3, NL 1
1943	Shibe Park, Philadelphia	AL 5, NL 3
1944	Forbes Field, Pittsburgh	NL 7, AL 1
1946	Fenway Park, Boston	AL 12, NL 0
1947	Wrigley Field, Chicago	AL 2. NL 1
1948	Sportsman's Park, St Louis	AL 5, NL 2
1949	Ebbets Field, Brooklyn	AL 11, NL 7
1950	Comiskey Park, Chicago	NL 4, AL 3
1951	Briggs Stadium, Detroit	NL 8, AL 3
1952	Shibe Park, Philadelphia	NL 3, AL 2
1953	Crosley Field, Cincinnati	NL 5, AL 1
1954	Municipal Stadium, Cleveland	AL 11, NL 9
1955	County Stadium, Milwaukee	NL 6, AL 5
1956	Griffith Stadium, Washington	NL 7, AL 3
1957	Busch Stadium, St Louis	AL 6, NL 5
1958	Memorial Stadium, Baltimore	AL 4, NL 3
1959, 1st	Forbes Field, Pittsburgh	NL 5, AL 4
, 2nd	Memorial Coliseum, Los Angeles	AL 5, NL 3
1960, 1st	Municipal Stadium, Kansas City	NL 5, AL 3
2nd	Yankee Stadium, New York	NL 6, AL 0
1961, 1st	Candlestick Park, San Francisco	NL 5, AL 4
2nd	Fenway Park, Boston	NL 1, AL 1
1962, 1st	D.C. Stadium, Washington	NL 3. AL 1
2nd	Wrigley Field, Chicago	AL 9, NL 4
1963	Municipal Stadium, Cleveland	NL 5, AL 3
1964	Shea Stadium, New York	NL 7, AL 4
1965	Metropolitan Stadium, Minnesota	NL 6, AL 5
1966	Busch Memorial Stadium, St Louis	NL 2, AL 1
1967	Anaheim Stadium, California	NL 2, AL 1
1968	Astrodome, Houston	NL 1, AL 0
1969	RFK Memorial Stadium, Washington	NL 9, AL 3
1970	Riverfront Stadium, Cincinnati	NL 5, AL 4
1971	Tiger Stadium, Detroit	AL 6, NL 4
1972	Atlanta Stadium, Atlanta	NL 4, AL 3
1973	Royals Stadium, Kansas City	NL 7, AL 1
1974	Three Rivers Stadium, Pittsburgh	NL 7, AL 2
1975	County Stadium, Milwaukee	NL 6, AL 3
1976	Veterans Stadium, Philadelphia	NL 7, AL 1
1977	Yankee Stadium, New York	NL 7, AL 5
1978	San Diego Stadium, San Diego	NL 7, AL 3
1979	Kingdome, Seattle	NL 7, AL 6
1980	Dodger Stadium, Los Angeles	NL 4, AL 2
1981	Municipal Stadium, Cleveland	NL 5, AL 4
1982	Olympic Stadium, Montreal	NL 4, AL 1
1983	Comiskey Park, Chicago	AL 13, NL 3
1984	Candlestick Park, San Francisco	NL 3, AL 1
1985	Metrodome, Minnesota	NL 6, AL 1
1986	Astrodome, Houston	AL 3, NL 2
1987	Oakland Coliseum, Oakland	
1988	Riverfront Stadium, Cincinnati	

NL has won 36, AL won 20, +1 tie, in the 57 games.

ALL-STAR TOUR OF JAPAN 1986

Twenty-four players representing nineteen of Major League baseball's twenty-six teams were invited to play seven games in Japan in November 1986, against a team of Japanese All-Stars.

The US squad was led by New York Mets manager Davey Johnson, still in seventh heaven from winning the 1986 World Series, with coaches Mel Stottlemyre of the Mets and Bobby Valentine, the successful Texas Rangers skipper.

The trip gave Johnson the opportunity to see old friends as he had played for the Yomuri Giants of Tokyo in 1975–76, as well as to thank Giants manager Shigeo Nagashina for bringing a welcome change of fortune to the Mets dugout when he dropped in to wish Johnson good luck before game 4 of the World Series.

Baseball was introduced to Japan in 1873 by Horace Wilson and had become the major summer sport in Japanese schools by the turn of the century. A tour by US All-Stars in 1908 helped promote the game, which also became established in the universities before the Second World War.

Professional baseball started in Japan in the mid-1930s following visits by two more squads of US All-Stars, which included Babe Ruth and Lou Gehrig. The two professional leagues (Pacific and Central) gained rapidly in popularity after the war, and the twelve clubs now draw a total of about 16 million spectators a year. The two league champions playoff each October in the Japan Series.

Twenty-two Americans played in Japan during 1987, including free agent Bob Horner who joined the Yakult Swallows from Atlanta for over $1.3m. A number of Major League teams have made end-of-season tours to Japan in recent years. The 1986 All-Star, Cal Ripken Jnr, played there with his club the Baltimore Orioles and was impressed by the standard of play. However, most players in the squad were making their first visit way out East and were particularly keen to do well.

The tour opened with four straight victories for the Americans but in the fifth game the Japanese All-Stars rallied in the eighth inning to win 6-4. Smarting from the unexpected loss, the Americans knuckled down to take the series by six games to one.

TOUR DETAILS

Game 1: 1 Nov. in Tokyo (34,000)
   USA 6 runs – 9 hits – 1 error
   Japan 3 runs – 9 hits – 2 errors
Game 2: 2 Nov. in Tokyo (47,000)
   USA 9 – 6 – 1 Japan 2 – 8 – 3
Game 3: 3 Nov. in Tokyo (30,000)
   Japan 0 – 3 – 1 USA 3 – 6 – 0
Game 4: 5 Nov. in Fukuoka (27,000)
   Japan 3 – 9 – 0 USA 13 – 17 – 1
Game 5: 6 Nov. in Osaka (32,000)
   Japan 6 – 10 – 0 USA 4 – 6 – 0
Game 6: 8 Nov. in Tokyo (27,000)
   USA 15 – 14 – 0 Japan 3 – 4 – 3
Game 7: 9 Nov. in Tokyo (37,000)
   USA 9 – 13 – 1 Japan 4 – 11 – 1

1986 All-Star Squad to Japan

Pitchers: John Franco (Reds), Greg Harris (Rangers), Willie Hernandez (Tigers), Teddy Higuera (Brewers), Jack Morris (Tigers), Jeff Reardon (Expos), Rick Rhoden (Pirates), Mike Scott (Astros), Mike Witt (Angels).
Catchers: Rich Gedman (Red Sox), Tony Pena (Pirates).
Infielders: Buddy Bell (Reds), Glenn Davis (Astros), Brook Jacoby (Indians), Wally Joyner (Angels), Cal Ripken Jr. (Orioles), Ryne Sandberg (Cubs), Ozzie Smith (Cardinals), Frank White (Royals).
Outfielders; Jesse Barfield (Blue Jays), Jose Canseco (Oakland As), Tony Gwynn (Padres), Von Hayes (Phillies), and Dale Murphy (Braves).
(A few players have since changed club.)

Right: U.S. All-Star Glenn Davis.

Far right: Jose Canseco learnt a great deal on tour in Japan.

AMERICAN LEAGUE CHAMPIONSHIP SERIES
HIGHLIGHTS 1969–86

When the two Major Leagues each divided into two divisions it was decided that the winner of the East should play the winner of the West in a best of five games playoff. This was expanded, somewhat controversially, into the best of seven games in 1985. Some people had misgivings about the league pennant playoffs being the same length as the World Series, while others were fearful that by extending the post-season still later into autumn, it was only a matter of time before an already chilly World Series night game would be postponed because of ice or snowy weather.

The 1972 ALCS was packed with drama, suspense, and too much bad behaviour from fans and players alike. Oakland won the first two games at home but were swept aside in game 3 in Detroit by pitcher Joe Coleman's fourteen strikeouts. In game 4, Oakland were leading 3–1 after 10½ innings but a bases-loaded walk to Norm Cash and a hit to right field by Jim Northrup levelled the playoffs at two games all. Despite the destructive distractions of the Detroit fans, Oakland took the pennant by winning the fifth and deciding game 2–1.

Oakland faced Baltimore in 1973 and again conceded a handy lead in game 4 to take the playoff to a fifth game. Surprisingly, only 24,265 fans turned up to see Oakland's star pitcher, Catfish Hunter, guide the As into another World Series.

The New York Yankees were strong favourites to beat Kansas City in the 1976 ALCS, but the Royals forced the playoff to a fifth game at Yankee Stadium. After six innings the New Yorkers led 6–3, but George Brett's three-run homer in the eighth brought KC back level. The score was still tied going into the bottom of the ninth inning when Yankees first baseman Chris Chambliss hit the first pitch from Mark Littell over the right field fence to win New York its first pennant since 1964. By the time Chambliss reached second base, thousands of fans had already invaded the field, tearing up $100,000 worth of 'souvenirs'.

The Yankees met the Royals again in 1977 and the playoff followed a similar script, with a fifth game necessary, this time in Kansas City (to the relief of the New York ground crew.) Tensions flared in the first inning when a fight erupted between George Brett and Graig Nettles. New York trailed 3–2 after eight innings, but when Royals pitcher Mark Littell was taken out of the game, Mickey Rivers and Willie Randolph drove in

two runs before the win was underlined by a run scored on a fielding error by George Brett.

In the top of the ninth inning in game 5 of the 1982 ALCS, Reggie Jackson (playing for the California Angels) was in the on-deck circle waiting for the chance to make one of his spectacular October contributions, but in the event he could only stand and watch in frustration as Milwaukee reliever Peter Ladd retired Rod Carew to win the game as the Brewers became the first team to win a pennant after losing the first two games.

For the 1985 playoffs the format was expanded to the best of seven games, which was just as well for Kansas City who trailed by three games to one. However, the Royals won the next three to sweep past the luckless Toronto Blue Jays and into the World Series.

The 1986 ALCS also went to seven games after the California Angels seemed to have the playoff sewn up. At one stage they were leading Boston by three games to one and ahead by 5–2 in the ninth inning, just one strike from winning the pennant, but lost 7–6. The game galvanised the Red Sox but seemed to break the Angels' spirit and they lost the last two games 10–4 and 8–1.

ALCS RESULTS

Year	Winner	Loser
1969	Baltimore (East), 3 games	Minnesota (West), 0 games
1970	Baltimore (East), 3	Minnesota (West), 0
1971	Baltimore (East), 3	Oakland (West), 0
1972	Oakland (West), 3	Detroit (East), 2
1973	Oakland (West), 3	Baltimore (East), 2
1974	Oakland (West), 3	Baltimore (East), 1 game
1975	Boston (East), 3	Oakland (West), 0
1976	New York (East), 3	Kansas City (West), 2
1977	New York (East), 3	Kansas City (West), 2
1978	New York (East), 3	Kansas City (West), 1 game
1979	Baltimore (East), 3	California (West), 1 game
1980	Kansas City (West), 3	New York (East), 0
1981	New York (East), 3	Oakland (West), 0
1982	Milwaukee (East), 3	California (West), 2
1983	Baltimore (East), 3	Chicago (West), 1 game
1984	Detroit (East), 3	Kansas City (West), 0
1985	Kansas City (West), 4	Toronto (East), 3
1986	Boston (East), 4	California (West), 3
1987		

Top right: Third baseman Wade Boggs played in all Boston's post-season games.

NATIONAL LEAGUE CHAMPIONSHIP SERIES
HIGHLIGHTS 1969–86

In the fifth and deciding game of the absorbing 1972 playoff, Pittsburgh led the Reds 3–2 going into the bottom of the ninth innings, and manager Bill Virdon brought the club's best pitcher, Dave Guisti, into the game to clinch the pennant. However, Cincinnati's Johnny Bench hit a home run over the right field fence to tie the score. Guisti gave up two more hits before being replaced by Bob Moose who got the Pirates within one out of winning but threw a pitch that bounced past the catcher, allowing pinch-runner George Foster to race home from third base to snatch the title.

Below: Catcher Gary Carter made vital hits for the Mets in the playoffs.

ALCS RECORDS 1969–86

Youngest player: 20 Claudell Washington, Oak 1974
Oldest player: 40 Reggie Jackson, Cal 1986
Most ALCS appearances: 11 Reggie Jackson
Most ALCS wins as manager: 4 Earl Weaver, Balt
Shortest game: 1hr 57 mins Balt-Oak 1974
Longest game: 3hrs 54 mins Cal-Bos 1986
Most innings played: 12 Balt-Min 1969
Highest game attendance: 64,406 Cal *v.* Milw 5 Oct 1982
Lowest game attendance: 24,265 Oak *v.* Balt 11 Oct 1973
Largest total ALCS attendance:
3 games 151,539 in 1981
4 games 195,748 in 1983
5 games 284,691 in 1982
6 games – none played
7 games 324,430 in 1986

The following year, the Reds fought out an ill-tempered playoff with the New York Mets. The trouble started when Cincinnati's Pete Rose ran into Mets fielder Bud Harrelson in an attempt to break up a double play. After a stormy few minutes the game continued but Rose was pelted with debris when he went out to field. In game 4, Rose gained his revenge for an unwelcome beer shower by hitting a home run in the twelfth to square the playoff at two games apiece, but the Mets won the deciding game 7–2.

The 1980 NLCS was a classic that had controversy, drama, recoveries, elation and despair in every game. In the deciding fifth game the Phillies trailed 5–2 after seven innings, recovered to 7–7 after eight, before winning 8–7.

The following year's playoff seemed as if it would be a one-sided affair because Los Angeles had beaten Montreal in eighteen of their last nineteen meetings. However, the Expos battled the Dodgers to a fifth game in chilly Montreal. The deciding game was postponed for a day because of sleety rain, and the cold certainly put the Dodgers at a disadvantage. The score was tied at 1–1 after eight innings, then Rick Monday hit a home run with two out in the top of the ninth which was enough for Los Angeles to squeeze past the Canadian team.

In the 1984 NLCS the Chicago Cubs were the popular favourites to win the pennant, and when they won the first two games 13–0 and 4–2 at Wrigley Field it seemed they would make it. However, San Diego levelled the playoff at two games each. In the final game, Chicago led 3–2 after six innings but a grounder through Leon Durham's legs off Rick Sutcliffe allowed the Padres to tie the game. Tony Gwynn and Steve Garvey then made crucial hits to give San Diego a 6–3 victory and their first pennant.

The following year, the playoff between Los Angeles and St Louis was expanded to the best of seven games. Each team won two games before the dramatic, if unlikely, events unfolded which settled the series. The Cards had hit less home runs than almost every other team during the regular season and in game 5, the Dodgers ace pitcher Fernando Valenzuela had cruised through eight innings, before being replaced by reliever Tom Niedenfuer in the ninth. Then, with the score 2–2, with one out in the bottom of the ninth inning, wizard shortstop Ozzie Smith hit a home run to give St Louis a 3–2 victory. In game 6, Los Angeles were leading 5–4 with two out in the top of the ninth, when Jack Clark hit a three-run homer off the luckless Neidenfuer to give the

Cardinals a winning 7–5 lead.

The 1986 playoffs only went to six games but it seemed like they played eight. Houston and New York won two games each before the Mets won game 5 in the bottom of the twelfth innings thanks to Gary Carter's second game-winning RBI of the playoffs. Game 6 went to sixteen innings, the longest post-season game ever, despite the Astros leading 3–0 after eight. New York levelled the game in the top of the ninth, and went ahead in the fourteenth, only to be pegged back once more. Ray Knight helped the Mets to a 7–4 lead after 15½ innings, but in a desperate finish, Houston were able to manage just two more runs before Mets reliever Jesse Orosco struck out Kevin Bass to grab his third win in the playoff.

NLCS RESULTS

Year	Winner	Loser
1969	New York (East), 3 games	Atlanta (West), 0 games
1970	Cincinnati (West), 3	Pittsburgh (East), 0
1971	Pittsburgh (East), 3	San Francisco (West), 1
1972	Cincinnati (West), 3	Pittsburgh (East), 2
1973	New York (East), 3	Cincinnati (West), 2
1974	Los Angeles (West), 3	Pittsburgh (East), 1
1975	Cincinnati (West), 3	Pittsburgh (East), 0
1976	Cincinnati (West), 3	Philadelphia (East), 0
1977	Los Angeles (West), 3	Philadelphia (East), 1
1978	Los Angeles (West), 3	Philadelphia (East), 1
1979	Pittsburgh (East), 3	Cincinnati (West), 0
1980	Philadelphia (East), 3	Houston (West), 2
1981	Los Angeles (West), 3	Montreal (East), 2
1982	St Louis (East), 3	Atlanta (West), 0
1983	Philadelphia (East), 3	Los Angeles (West), 1
1984	San Diego (West), 3	Chicago (East) 2
1985	St Louis (East), 4	Los Angeles (West), 2
1986	New York (East), 4	Houston (West), 2
1987		

NLCS RECORDS 1969–86

Youngest player: 21 Chris Speier, SF 1971
Oldest player: 42 Pete Rose, Phila 1983
Most NLCS appearances: 8 Richie Hebner
Most NLCS wins as manager: 4 Sparky Anderson, Cinc
Shortest game: 1hr 57 mins Pitts-Cinc 1972
Longest game: 4hrs 42 mins NY-Hous 1986
Most innings played: 12 NY-Hous 1986
Highest game attendance: 64,924 LA v. Phila 8 Oct 1977
Lowest game attendance: 33,088 Cinc v. Pitts 3 Oct 1970
Largest total NLCS attendances:
3 games 180,338 in 1976
4 games 240,584 in 1977
5 games 264,950 in 1980
6 games 326,824 in 1985
7 games – none played

THE WORLD SERIES 1903–86

The first official World Series between the champion clubs of the National and American Leagues was played in 1903, but about twenty years previously the American Association had challenged the more established National League to an end-of-season World Championship.

These playoffs took place from 1884 until the American Association folded in 1890, and although the NL clubs held the upper hand in most encounters, the St Louis Browns defeated the Chicago White Stockings in 1886.

The National League also looked down its nose at the newly-formed American League but in 1903 the NL champions, the Pittsburgh Pirates (who celebrated their centenary in 1987), agreed to play the Boston Pilgrims (who became the Red Sox) in a post-season series, but lost 5–4. Despite press and public protests, the New York Giants refused to play Boston the following year, but had to play the Philadelphia Athletics in 1905.

The Athletics, without their star pitcher Rube Waddell, had no answer to the young Giants right-hander Christy Mathewson, who won three games in just six days. Despite this setback to its credibility, the 'junior circuit', as the American League became known, went on to win six of the first ten series, and eighteen of the first thirty. The triumphs and disasters of the game's best players soon established the end-of-season Classic as America's premier sporting event.

In mid-July 1914, Boston's 'Miracle' Braves were last in the AL, but recovered to win the League and the Series.

Two years later, Babe Ruth pitched fourteen innings for the Boston Red Sox, and collected two more wins in 1918. Ruth was later sold to the New York Yankees who harnessed his blossoming hitting ability to help the club win three of their six series appearances in the 1920s, and five more in the 1930s. (Ruth hit three home runs in one game in 1926 and again two years later.)

One of the most remarkable games during that period was game 4 in 1929, when Philadelphia were losing 8–0 to the Chicago Cubs after 6½ innings but ended up winning 10–8.

Ten years later, the Yankees were grabbing the headlines as rookie Charlie Keller had a brilliant series, standing in for ailing superstar Lou Gehrig, to give the New York club its fourth title in a row.

In 1954, Willie Mays marked his return to the New York Giants from the US Army by saving game 1 of the Series with one of his speciality over-the-shoulder catches. Then inspired teammate Dusty Rhodes came off the bench to help win the first three games with his hitting.

Records galore were set in 1956, as the Yankees, led by Mickey Mantle playing in his first series, recovered to beat their cross-town rivals the Brooklyn Dodgers. This series is best remembered for pitcher Don Larsen's perfect game, in which he retired twenty-seven consecutive Brooklyn batters:

In 1960 the all-round brilliance of Bobby Richardson and the powerful Yankees batters enabled them to win three of the first four games by wide margins, but the Pittsburgh Pirates won the Series thanks to Bill Mazeroski's dramatic home run in the ninth inning of the seventh and deciding game.

Eight years later, the Detroit Tigers pitcher Mickey Lolich won three games and hit his first ever home run to steal the thunder from teammate Denny McLain, and St Louis ace Bob Gibson who had struck out seventeen Tigers in game 1.

The 1969 Series proved that fairy tales sometimes come true when, as if by the wave of a magic wand, the New York Mets, who had been the team that New Yorkers flocked to watch lose, suddenly leapt from last in their division to win the NL pennant and the Series.

Baltimore Orioles third baseman Brooks Robinson ensured his team won in 1970 with some solid hitting and brilliant fielding. The next year another all-time great, Roberto Clemente, inspired his Pittsburgh club to victory.

From 1972–74 the feuding Oakland As, who had little in common except their moustaches and their dislike of owner Charles O. Finley, won three Series in a row.

The 1975 Series was a classic, and perhaps the only one in living memory to top 1986. In seven games that had just about everything, Johnny Bench and Pete Rose led the Cincinnati 'Big Red Machine' to victory over the Boston Red Sox.

The most recent club to win back-to-back series has been the New York Yankees. In 1977, 'Mr October' Reggie Jackson repeated his Oakland heroics for the New Yorkers with three home runs in game 6 against Los Angeles.

Two years later, Willie 'Pops' Stargell's Pittsburgh family repeated their script of 1971 to win after trailing 3–1.

In 1980, the Philadelphia Phillies won the franchise's first series after ninety-seven years in the National League, and in 1985 an expansion club, the Kansas City Royals, recovered from losing the first two games at home to take America's most prestigious team championship, the World Series of professional baseball.

1986 WORLD SERIES

The New York Mets had been overwhelming during the regular season but only just squeezed past the Houston Astros and into the 1986 World Series. Their starting and relief pitchers were in great form, but the batters were in a slump, having hit a club average of just .189 in the NLCS.

The Boston Red Sox were content to be the clear World Series underdogs and determined to show that their hitters were under-rated by the arrogant NL champions, and to embarrass further those pundits who thought the club would finish near the foot of the AL East.

As in 1985, the pressure for high TV ratings meant that every game was played at night. While this may be good for advertisers it prevents young children watching the drama unfold and makes the players keep particularly late hours.

In the first game of the 1986 World Series, Boston's starting pitcher Bruce Hurst and reliever Calvin Schiraldi combined to shut out the Mets, while the Red Sox batters squeezed just four hits in a 1–0 victory decided by a mistake.

The only run came in the seventh inning when Jim Rice led off with a walk against Mets starter Ron Darling. He went to second base on a wild pitch, then scored when Rich Gedman's grounder went through reserve second baseman Tim Teufel's legs and into right field.

Game 1: Saturday, 18 October 1986,
at Shea Stadium, New York. Start: 8.28pm.
Boston   000 000 100 – 1 5 0*
New York   000 000 000 – 0 4 1
Hurst, Schiraldi (9) and Gedman, Bos.;
Darling, McDowell (8) and Carter, NY.
W-Hurst 1–0, L-Darling 0–1. HR-none.
LOB-Bos. 8, NY 8
GWRBI-none.
Time: 2.59 Att: 55,076

*See p. 125 for an explanation of these line scores.

In game 2, the Red Sox batters sprayed eighteen hits around Shea Stadium off five Mets pitchers to win the game 9–3. Boston scored three runs in the third inning, then Mets starting pitcher Dwight Gooden gave up a fourth inning home run to Dave Henderson and another in the fifth to Dwight Evans. Boston's star pitcher Roger Clemens was replaced in the fifth inning by relievers Steve Crawford and Bob Stanley who soon stopped the possibility of any Mets revival.

Game 2: Sunday, 19 October 1986,
at Shea Stadium, New York. Start: 8.25pm.
Boston   003 120 201 – 9 18 0
New York   002 010 000 – 3 8 1
Clemens, Crawford (5), Stanley (7) and Gedman, Bos.;
Gooden, Aguilera (6), Orosco (7), Fernandez (9),
Sisk (9) and Carter, NY. W-Crawford 1–0, Sv-Stanley.
L-Gooden 0–1, HR-Henderson, Evans, Bos.
LOB-Bos. 13, NY 9.
GWRBI-Boggs, Bos.
Time: 3.36 Att: 55,063

The Mets got off to a great start in game 3, at Boston, with Lenny Dykstra's lead-off home run and RBIs by Gary Carter and Danny Heep off pitcher Dennis Boyd, which gave New York a 4–0 lead. Mets starter Bob Ojeda held his former teammates to just one run and five hits in seven innings, then reliever Roger McDowell retired all six Red Sox batters he faced. To seal in the victory, New York added two runs in the seventh and another in the eighth.

Game 3: Tuesday, 21 October 1986,
at Fenway Park, Boston. Start: 8.28pm.
New York   400 000 210 – 7 13 0
Boston   001 000 000 – 1 5 0
Ojeda, McDowell (8) and Carter, NY.; Boyd,
Sambito (8), Stanley (8) and Gedman, Bos.
W-Ojeda 1–0, L-Boyd 0–1. HR-Dykstra, NY.
LOB-NY 6, Bos. 6.
GWRBI-Dykstra, NY.
Time: 2.58 Att: 33,595

Gary Carter's two home runs and starting pitcher Ron Darling's seven-inning shutout ensured the Mets won game 4 and tied the World Series at two games all. In the fourth inning, Carter hit a two-run homer off Boston starter Al Nipper, then smacked the ball over the left field screen in the eighth. Meanwhile, Lenny Dykstra had scored his second series homer, off Crawford, in the seventh. For Boston, only Gedman, with three hits, got the measure of Darling and reliever Jesse Orosco.

Game 4: Wednesday, 22 October 1986,
at Fenway Park, Boston. Start: 8.25pm.
New York   000 300 210 – 6 12 0
Boston   000 000 020 – 2 7 1
Darling, McDowell (8), Orosco (8) and Carter, NY.;
Nipper, Crawford (9), Stanley (9) and Gedman, Bos.
W-Darling 1–1, Sv-Orosco, L-Nipper 0–1.
HR-Carter 2, Dykstra, NY. GWRBI-Carter, NY.
LOB-NY 4, Bos. 11.
Time: 3.22 Att: 33,920

The Red Sox scored the first home win in the 1986 World Series in game 5, thanks to the pitching of their starter Bruce Hurst. Boston scored through RBIs from Dwight Evans, Dave Henderson and Don Baylor and a sacrifice fly ball by Spike Owen, to give Dwight Gooden his second defeat of the series. The Mets finally scored thanks to Tim Teufel's home run in the eighth inning and Rafael Santana's RBI single in the ninth.

Game 5: Thursday, 23 October 1986,
at Fenway Park, Boston. Start: 8.39pm.
New York   000 000 011 – 2 10 1
Boston   011 020 00x – 4 12 0
Gooden, Fernandez (5) and Carter, NY. Hurst
and Gedman, Bos. W-Hurst 2–0, L-Gooden 0–2.
HR-Teufel, NY. GWRBI-Owen, Bos.
LOB-NY 8, Bos. 11.
Time: 3.09 Att: 34,010

In one of the most exciting games in World Series history, Boston took an early 2–0 lead off Mets starter Bob Ojeda in game 6. Red Sox ace Roger Clemens kept the Mets scoreless until the fifth inning when an RBI single by Ray Knight and a grounder by Danny Heep tied the score. Boston went ahead 3–2 on Dwight Evan's grounder off Roger McDowell in the seventh inning, but the Mets made the score 3–3 in the eighth, thanks to a sacrifice fly by Gary Carter off reliever Calvin Schiraldi.

The Mets and Red Sox were never far apart throughout the Series.

With the score tied after nine, the game went to extra innings. Dave Henderson led off the Boston tenth with a home run over the left field fence off Rick Aguilera who then gave up an RBI single to Marty Barrett and Boston went into the bottom of the tenth leading 5–3.

Schiraldi dismissed Wally Backman and Keith Hernandez but Gary Carter and pinch hitter Kevin Mitchell got on base with singles. Schiraldi then threw two strikes to Mets third baseman Ray Knight to put Boston just one strike away from the team's first World Series since 1918. However, Knight singled into centre field allowing Carter to score and sending Mitchell to third base. Bob Stanley replaced Schiraldi on the mound and threw two balls and two strikes to the next Mets batter, Mookie Wilson. As the tension rose, Wilson fouled off two pitches. Then Stanley threw a wild pitch which enabled Mitchell to score the tying run. After fouling off two more pitches, Wilson hit a ground ball trickling towards first baseman Bill Buckner, but it went through his legs into right field, allowing Ray Knight to score the winning run.

Game 6: Saturday, 25 October 1986,
at Shea Stadium, New York. Start: 8.25pm.
Boston   110 000 100 2 – 5 13 3
New York   000 020 010 3 – 6 8 2
Clemens, Schiraldi (8), Stanley (10) and Gedman,
Bos.; Ojeda, McDowell (7), Orosco (8), Aguilera (9)
and Carter, NY. W-Aguilera 1–0, L-Schiraldi 0–1.
LOB-Bos. 14, NY 8.
HR-none, GWRBI-none.
Time: 4.02 Att: 55,078

After a day's delay because of rain, Boston soon snapped out of their state of shock in game 7, with second inning home runs by Dwight Evans and Rich Gedman and an RBI single by Wade Boggs off Ron Darling. Sid Fernandez replaced Darling in the fourth and soon dismissed seven Red Sox in a row. The Mets batters did not get to grips with Boston's starter Bruce Hurst until the sixth inning when they tied the score 3–3. Series MVP Ray Knight led off the seventh with a home run off reliever Schiraldi which was followed by an RBI single by Rafael Santana and a sacrifice fly by Keith Hernandez to give the Mets a 6–3 lead. Boston closed the gap in the eighth with Dwight Evans' two-run homer off Roger McDowell, but Darryl Strawberry's eighth inning home run off Al Nipper and an RBI single by pitcher Jesse Orosco re-established the three-run cushion. When Orosco struck out Marty Barrett to end the game, the New York Mets had won their second World Series, and became only the second team (Kansas City was first in 1985) to take the title after losing their first two games at home.

Game 7: Monday, 27 October 1986, at Shea Stadium, New York. Start: 8.25pm.

Boston	030 000 020 – 5	9	0
New York	000 003 32x – 8	10	0

Hurst, Schiraldi (7), Sambito (7), Stanley (7), Nipper (8), Crawford (8) and Gedman, Bos.; Darling, Fernandez (4), McDowell (7), Orosco (8) and Carter, NY. W-McDowell 1–0, L-Schiraldi 0–2. Sv-Orosco. LOB-Bos. 6, NY 7. HR-Evans, Gedman, Bos. GWRBI-Knight, NY. Time: 3.11 Att: 55,032

WORLD SERIES 1986 STATISTICS

Team records	New York–Boston	
Games won	4	3
At bats	240	248
Runs	32	27
Hits	65	69
Home runs	7	5
Runs batted in	29	26
Left on base	50	69
Stolen bases	7	0
Team average	.271	.278
Put outs	189	188
Errors	5	4
Innings pitched	63	62
Earned run average	3.29	4.31
Strikeouts	53	43
Bases on balls	28	21
Total/(average) time	23h.17m	(3h.19m)
Total/(average) att.	321,774	(45,968)
Gate receipts	$10.4m (record)	

METS ON BROADWAY

The New York Mets players and their families had good reason to smile and wave throughout their sunny parade down Broadway the day after their victory in the 1986 World Series. Not only had they been involved in the most dramatic series since 1975, attracted a record TV audience for a baseball game of 80 million, they had also been awarded a record payout share of $86,254 each.

The traditional parade began at Battery Park and slowly wound its way for a mile or so up Broadway to City Hall Plaza, the route America's heroes have driven in triumph for sixty years, since solo flyer Charles Lindberg's parade.

The crowd of about one million New Yorkers cheered and waved while office workers threw shredded computer printouts and ripped up telephone directories from skyscraper windows onto the jammed street below. When the victory parade was over, New York's rubbish men swept up about 650 tons of debris (3,400 tons were collected after astronaut John Glenn's parade in 1962, and a record 5,400 tons after the V-J Day parade in 1945).

WORLD SERIES RESULTS AND ATTENDANCE FIGURES

Year	Winner Games	Loser Games	Games	Total
1903	Boston AL, 5	Pittsburgh NL, 3	8	100,429
1904	No Series			
1905	New York NL, 4	Philadelphia AL, 1	5	91,723
1906	Chicago AL, 4	Chicago NL, 2	6	99,845
1907	Chicago NL, 4	Detroit AL, 0; (1 tie)	5	78,068
1908	Chicago NL, 4	Detroit AL, 1	5	62,232
1909	Pittsburgh NL, 4	Detroit AL, 3	7	145,295
1910	Philadelphia AL, 4	Chicago NL, 1	5	124,222
1911	Philadelphia AL, 4	New York NL, 2	6	179,851
1912	Boston AL, 4	New York NL, 3; (1 tie)	8	252,037
1913	Philadelphia AL, 4	New York NL, 1	5	151,000
1914	Boston NL, 4	Philadelphia AL, 0	4	111,009
1915	Boston AL, 4	Philadelphia NL, 1	5	143,351
1916	Boston AL, 4	Brooklyn NL, 1	5	162,859
1917	Chicago AL, 4	New York NL, 2	6	186,654
1918	Boston AL, 4	Chicago NL, 2	6	128,483
1919	Cincinnati NL, 5	Chicago AL, 3	8	236,928
1920	Cleveland AL, 5	Brooklyn NL, 2	7	178,737
1921	New York NL, 5	New York AL, 3	8	269,976
1922	New York NL, 4	New York AL, 0; (1 tie)	5	185,947
1923	New York AL, 4	New York NL, 2	6	301,430
1924	Washington AL, 4	New York NL, 3	7	283,665
1925	Pittsburgh NL, 4	Washington AL, 3	7	282,848
1926	St Louis NL, 4	New York AL, 3	7	328,051
1927	New York AL, 4	Pittsburgh NL, 0	4	201,705
1928	New York AL, 4	St Louis NL, 0	4	199,072
1929	Philadelphia AL, 4	Chicago NL, 1	5	190,490
1930	Philadelphia AL, 4	St Louis NL, 2	6	212,619
1931	St Louis NL, 4	Philadelphia AL, 3	7	231,567
1932	New York AL, 4	Chicago NL, 0	4	191,998
1933	New York NL, 4	Washington AL, 1	5	163,076
1934	St Louis NL, 4	Detroit AL, 3	7	281,510
1935	Detroit AL, 4	Chicago NL, 2	6	286,672
1936	New York AL, 4	New York NL, 2	6	302,924
1937	New York AL, 4	New York NL, 1	5	238,142
1938	New York AL, 4	Chicago NL, 0	4	200,833
1939	New York AL, 4	Cincinnati NL, 0	4	183,849
1940	Cincinnati NL, 4	Detroit AL, 3	7	281,927
1941	New York AL, 4	Brooklyn NL, 1	5	235,773
1942	St Louis NL, 4	New York AL, 1	5	277,101
1943	New York AL, 4	St Louis NL, 1	5	277,312
1944	St Louis NL, 4	St Louis AL, 2	6	206,708
1945	Detroit AL, 4	Chicago NL, 3	7	333,457
1946	St Louis NL, 4	Boston AL, 3	7	250,071
1947	New York AL, 4	Brooklyn NL, 3	7	389,763
1948	Cleveland AL, 4	Boston NL, 2	6	358,362
1949	New York AL, 4	Brooklyn NL, 1	5	236,716
1950	New York AL, 4	Philadelphia NL, 0	4	196,009
1951	New York AL, 4	New York NL, 2	6	341,977
1952	New York AL, 4	Brooklyn NL, 3	7	340,706
1953	New York AL, 4	Brooklyn NL, 2	6	307,350
1954	New York NL, 4	Cleveland AL, 0	4	251,507
1955	Brooklyn NL, 4	New York AL, 3	7	362,310
1956	New York AL, 4	Brooklyn NL, 3	7	345,903
1957	Milwaukee NL, 4	New York AL, 3	7	394,712
1958	New York AL, 4	Milwaukee NL, 3	7	393,909
1959	Los Angeles NL, 4	Chicago AL, 2	7	420,784
1960	Pittsburgh NL, 4	New York AL, 3	7	349,813
1961	New York AL, 4	Cincinnati NL, 1	5	223,247
1962	New York AL, 4	San Francisco NL, 3	7	376,864
1963	Los Angeles NL, 4	New York AL, 0	4	247,279
1964	St Louis NL, 4	New York AL, 3	7	321,807
1965	Los Angeles NL, 4	Minnesota AL, 3	7	364,326
1966	Baltimore AL, 4	Los Angeles NL, 0	4	220,791
1967	St Louis NL, 4	Boston AL, 3	7	304,085
1968	Detroit AL, 4	St Louis NL, 3	7	379,670
1969	New York NL, 4	Baltimore AL, 1	5	272,378
1970	Baltimore AL, 4	Cincinnati NL, 1	5	253,183
1971	Pittsburgh NL, 4	Baltimore AL, 3	7	351,091
1972	Oakland AL, 4	Cincinnati NL, 3	7	363,149
1973	Oakland AL, 4	New York NL, 3	7	358,289
1974	Oakland AL, 4	Los Angeles NL, 1	5	260,004
1975	Cincinnati NL, 4	Boston AL, 3	7	308,272
1976	Cincinnati NL, 4	New York AL, 0	4	223,009
1977	New York AL, 4	Los Angeles NL, 2	6	337,708
1978	New York AL, 4	Los Angeles NL, 2	6	337,304
1979	Pittsburgh NL, 4	Baltimore AL, 3	7	367,597
1980	Philadelphia NL, 4	Kansas City AL, 2	6	324,516
1981	Los Angeles NL, 4	New York AL, 2	6	338,081
1982	St Louis NL, 4	Milwaukee AL, 3	7	384,570
1983	Baltimore AL, 4	Philadelphia NL, 1	5	304,139
1984	Detroit AL, 4	San Diego NL, 1	5	271,820
1985	Kansas City AL, 4	St Louis NL, 3	7	327,494
1986	New York NL, 4	Boston AL, 3	7	321,774
1987				

Above: The Mets win Game 7 and the 1986 celebrations begin.
Left: Mets outfielder, Mookie Wilson.

WORLD SERIES RECORDS 1903–86
TEAM RECORDS

AL clubs won 48: won 267 games, scored 354 home runs (12 in 1956).
NL clubs won 35: won 223 games, scored 249 home runs (9 in 1977 and 1955).
36 teams have won WS after losing the first game.
10 teams have won WS after losing two games.
6 teams have won WS after winning one but losing three games.
No team has ever won WS after losing the first three games.

Latest date WS started: 20 October 1981.
Latest date WS finished: 28 October 1981.
Most innings played, day game: 14, in 1916.
Most innings played, night game: 12, in 1977 and 1975.
Shortest game: 1hr 25mins in 1908.
Longest game: 4hrs 13mins in 1973.
First night game: Pitts v. Balt 13 Oct 1971.
All seven WS games at night: 1985 and 1986.
Highest game attendance: 92,706 LA v. Chic 6 Oct 1959.
Most runs scored by a team: 18, by NY Yankees 2 Oct 1936.

RECORDS BY PLAYERS IN A GAME

Most hits: 5 Paul Molitor 1982.
Most runs: 4 (5 players, 1977 most recent).
Most RBIs: 6 Bobby Richardson 1960.
Most home runs: 3 Babe Ruth 1927 and 1928, Reggie Jackson 1977.
Most stolen bases: 3 (4 times, 1968 most recent).
Most strikeouts by pitcher: 17 Bob Gibson 1968.
Perfect game by a pitcher: Don Larsen 8 October 1956.
12 occasions players have hit grand slam home runs (1970 most recent).
12 occasions players have stolen home to score (1964 most recent).

RECORDS BY PLAYERS IN A SERIES OR CAREER

Most WS as a player: 14 Yogi Berra (won 10 of them).
Most WS as a manager: 10 Casey Stengel (won 7 of them).
Most WS as an umpire: 18 Bill Klem (104 games).
Youngest player: 18yrs 10m 3 days Fred Lindstrom 1924.
Oldest player: 46yrs 2m 29 days John Quinn 1930.
Oldest non-pitcher: 42yrs 6m 2 days Pete Rose 1983.
Youngest manager: 26yrs 11m 21 days Joe Cronin, Wash 1933.

Top Six Batting Averages in WS:

.625 Babe Ruth 1928
.545 Henry Gowdy 1914
.545 Lou Gehrig 1928
.533 Johnny Bench 1976
.529 Lou Gehrig 1932
.529 Thurman Munson 1976

Top Six Total Home Runs:

18 Mickey Mantle (12 WS)
15 Babe Ruth (10 WS)
12 Yogi Berra (14 WS)
11 Ed Snider (6 WS)
10 Lou Gehrig (7 WS)
10 Reggie Jackson (5 WS)

CLIMBING THE MAJOR LEAGUE MOUNTAIN

Today's would-be Major Leaguers, who play for one of the many organisations which provide baseball leagues and tournaments for young people (such as Little League or Pony League), usually follow one of two courses when they leave high school.

The traditional way has been to be signed by a Major League club and then sent to one of its four or five Minor League 'farm' teams to improve their technique and learn the club's system of play.

The farm system was developed over fifty years ago, by Major League administrators such as Branch Rickey and George Weiss, so that a franchise would have a steady stream of talented young players under contract, who would in time either play in the majors, or be traded to another team for one of its players.

Once ready for a better standard of baseball, youngsters would move up through the Minor Leagues from Rookie Leagues, to AA, then AAA, until ready to be called up to the Major League roster.

There are now about 3,500 players at nearly 150 Minor League teams around the country. The best of them, such as Louisville of the American Association, have been known to draw more fans in a season than a couple of the Major League teams.

The following list shows the framework of the Minor League system.

AAA: International League (8 clubs) started 1884
       American Association (8) 1902
       Pacific Coast League (10) 1903
       Mexican Summer League (16) 1955
AA: Texas League (8) 1888
       Southern League (10) 1904
       Eastern League (8) 1923
A: Northwest League (8) 1901
       California League (10) 1914
       Florida State League (14) 1919
       New York-Pennsylvania League (12) 1939
       Carolina League (8) 1945
       Midwest League (12) 1947
       South Atlantic League (12) 1948
Rookie Leagues (Summer A):   Appalachian 1921
                                          Pioneer 1939
                                          Gulf Coast 1964

All but four of the clubs, (less those in the Mexican Summer League), are owned or otherwise linked with a Major League franchise.

In the 1920s, players such as Lou Gehrig and Eddie Collins from Columbia U., who went into the Major Leagues from college, were something of an exception. Today, over 60 per cent of Major Leaguers went from high school to college. This meant that they not only played amateur NCAA (National Collegiate Athletic Association) baseball but also gained an educational qualification which might help them when they finish playing the game.

The College World Series started in 1947 and this extra competition has helped the standard of NCAA baseball improve rapidly. Some of the many modern college stadiums being built around the country have excellent playing and training facilities. The 1987 CWS was won by Stanford University.

Thirteen of the twenty college players who were on the USA silver medal winning team at the 1984 Olympic Games baseball tournament have since played in the Major Leagues.

Although the majority of players drafted by Major League teams spend a couple of years with an AA or AAA farm club, exceptional athletes (such as Kansas City's Bo Jackson) are able to make the transition from AA to the big leagues in about a season.

FROM ESSEX TO FLORIDA

In early February 1987, twenty-five-year-old Essex County cricketer Ian Pont flew to Philadelphia with his brother Keith (who played for Essex for sixteen seasons) on the first stage of a whistle-stop tour of eight Major League baseball clubs, in his quest to become a big-league pitcher.

Ian has had an interest in baseball for some years, and during the winter of 1986, while coaching cricket in South Africa, played baseball for Durban Vikings, and was helped for several weeks by ex-Springbok coach Jimmy Pershouse.

His progress as a rookie pitcher was startling. After winning his first start for the 'B' team, he was promoted to the 'A' side and won that as well. After a month he was called into the Natal squad for inter-provincial matches. Although he did not play, Ian's power on the mound impressed everyone.

Ian is well known on the county cricket circuit for his strong throwing arm but is cautious about putting figures to his impressive pitching speed.

Ian had spring training tryouts with the Philadelphia Phillies, Texas Rangers, Los Angeles Dod-gers, Houston Astros, Chicago White Sox, Cleveland Indians, Toronto Blue Jays and the New York Yankees. These ranged from ten-minutes throwing in front of cold, bored coaches to an extensive trial with the Phillies. The coaches seemed impressed with Ian's potential and at one stage it seemed they might send him to either Clearwater or Spartanburg, the club's A grade farm clubs, but it was not to be; at least, not in 1987.

Ian was not the only pitcher the Phillies let go that day. They also released future Hall of Famer Steve Carlton.

A winter of Aussie baseball and cricket may help Ian Pont into the majors.

AMATEUR BASEBALL

The October 1986 IOC meeting in Lausanne is probably best remembered in Britain for the decision not to award the 1992 summer games to Birmingham. But to baseball fans and players around the world it was the great occasion when baseball was included as the 25th Summer Olympic sport. Baseball's first full Olympic medals will be awarded in 1992 at Barcelona, Spain.

For the past eighty years baseball has been a popular demonstration sport at seven Olympiads: 1904 St Louis; 1912 Stockholm; 1936 Berlin (where 125,000 watched the USA World Amateurs beat the USA Olympics 6–5); 1952 Helsinki; 1956 Melbourne (over 100,000 saw the USA defeat Australia 11–5 at the Melbourne Cricket Ground); and in 1964 at Tokyo.

The 1984 demonstration tournament was won by Japan and attracted 385,290 spectators to Dodger Stadium, Los Angeles, making baseball the fourth most popular sport of the Games.

At the 24th modern Olympiad in 1988 at Seoul, South Korea, baseball's final demonstration tournament will be held at the modern, 50,000 capacity Chamshil Baseball Stadium in the heart of the Olympic complex.

Baseball is the premier spectator sport in South Korea, so Olympic officials have high hopes that the competition will be as successful as the tournament in Los Angeles.

The competition will involve eight nations, four of which (South Korea, Japan, Cuba, and Australia) will qualify automatically. The other four teams will be the 1987 CEBA Champion, the best two teams at the 1987 Pan-Am Games (excluding Cuba) and, finally, the winner of a playoff in Cuba at the InterContinental Cup between the 1987 CEBA runner-up and the third placed team at the 1987 Pan-Am Games (again, excluding Cuba).

There are already four baseball fields in Barcelona which could be used for Olympic competition in 1992. CEBA's 1987 Pool 'A' Championships gave officials an ideal opportunity to see what improvements were necessary. The tentative arrangement made at the 1986 IOC meeting was that just six nations would be involved, although IBA officials hope this may be expanded to more than eight teams. One place will be reserved for the host country (Spain); the 1991 CEBA Pool 'A' Champions (probably Italy or the Netherlands) may have to playoff against the African Champions (probably Tunisia) for the second place. Two teams would be drawn from Asia/Oceania (Taiwan, South Korea, Japan or Australia); and two teams from the Americas (Cuba, USA, Puerto Rico or Venezuela).

As may be seen from this list, a number of extremely strong baseball teams will not make it to Barcelona. Indeed, unless baseball goes 'open' as an Olympic sport, it is by no means certain that the USA, the country which introduced baseball to so many, will qualify for the tournament, let alone win the coveted first Olympic gold medal.

The world governing body of amateur baseball is the IBA (International Baseball Association), which has its modern headquarters in Indianapolis, Indiana, USA. Sixty-two national federations representing countries in every continent are already members of the IBA, and at least a dozen other nations, including the USSR, are on the point of affiliating or forming federations.

The Association's much travelled President, Dr Bob Smith, of Greenville, Illinois, expects membership to exceed 100 countries before the turn of the century.

Federations in Europe, such as the newly reconstituted BBF in Britain (formerly the BABSF), also affiliate to CEBA (the European Amateur Baseball Confederation). This organisation recently celebrated its Silver Jubilee, and is run by Secretary-General Roger Panaye from its headquarters in Belgium.

One of the IBA's current plans is to encourage 'T' ball, a version of baseball suitable for young children, all around the world. IBA officials hope that Britain will become one of the first countries to benefit from the scheme.

The 1986 review of European baseball by CEBA listed its eighteen member nations in order of total players (the date in brackets shows when each federation was formed):

1. Italy	(1950)	13,250
2. The Netherlands	(1912)	12,280
3. France	(1914)	6,090
4. Spain	(1944)	4,304
5. W. Germany	(1955)	2,050
6. Belgium	(1936)	1,386
7. Denmark	(1978)	680
8. Britain	(1890)	610
9. Sweden	(1956)	585
10. Yugoslavia	(1982)	469
11. Poland	(1957)	453
12. Malta	(1982)	439
13. Czechoslovakia	(1964)	380
14. Tunisia	(1982)	314
15. Switzerland	(1981)	305
16. San Marino	(1970)	164
17. Finland	(1981)	162
18. Austria	(1983)	48

20TH EUROPEAN CHAMPIONSHIPS, POOL 'A', JULY 1987 in Spain

The Netherlands	Spain
Italy	San Marino
Belgium	West Germany,
Sweden	and France

MAJOR IBA & CEBA TOURNAMENTS IN 1987–88

CEBA Pool 'A' Championship 17–26 July 1987 Barcelona

Asian Championship August 1987 Tokyo

Pan-Am Games 7–23 August 1987 Indianapolis

8th InterContinental Cup 11–16 October 1987 Havana

CEBA Pool 'B' Championship mid-August 1988 Britain

30th World Championship 26 August–7 September 1988 Italy

Olympic Games 17 September–2 October 1988 Seoul

The InterContinental Cup and World Championships are held in alternate years, as are the CEBA Pool 'A' and Pool 'B' Championships.

BASEBALL IN BRITAIN

One of the earliest references to the term baseball does not come from America but is found in *A Little Pretty Pocket Book*, an alphabet of twenty-six children's games published in London in 1744. The letter 'B' is represented by Base-Ball, but the woodcut picture seems, to modern eyes, more like stoolball than baseball.

Baseball was certainly a well-connected game, as just four years later, Lady Hervey wrote to the effect that Frederick, Prince of Wales, would waste his time playing the schoolboys' game of base-ball. Fifty years later, it was still considered a children's game; Jane Austen (who rarely travelled beyond the southern counties of England) wrote near the beginning of her novel *Northanger Abbey* that the young heroine, Catherine, preferred cricket and base ball to books.

In 1834, Robin Carver wrote an American edition of *The Boys Own Book*, first published in London in 1828. The original included details about rounders and feeder, but in Carver's book, published in Boston, Massachusetts, the section was renamed base or goal ball.

Twelve years later baseball was codified by New Yorker Alexander J. Cartwright, and its growth and development becomes easier to trace. In 1874, two American professional baseball teams toured England and Ireland playing fourteen baseball and seven cricket matches at venues which included Lord's Cricket Ground and Kennington Oval. On a world tour by US All-Stars in 1889, several matches were played in England, Scotland and Ireland. The Prince of Wales watched the first game at the Oval.

In 1890, the Baseball Association of Great Britain and Ireland was formed, as was the National League of Professional Baseball Clubs of Great Britain, financed by A. G. Spalding. Three football clubs, Preston North End, Aston Villa and Stoke, formed teams which competed for the Spalding Cup. The main centres of baseball at the time were Derby, London, Tyneside and Teesside.

Early in 1914, the New York Giants and Chicago White Sox played a game at Stamford Bridge, watched by King George V, and the same teams returned ten years later to play a series of exhibition matches around the country. The attendance of George V, Queen Mary, the Prince of Wales and Prince Henry at the last game of the tour at Stamford Bridge is marked by a plaque which may still be seen at Chelsea's ground.

In the early 1920s a short-lived league was organised by the American Legion. When that folded, the London Americans played for many years against a variety of scratch sides, many made up of American entertainers appearing in London or the crews of American ships.

In 1933, Littlewoods Pools tycoon John Moores popularised baseball in the Merseyside area, then extended his efforts to Manchester, Birmingham, Yorkshire, London and South Wales. A number of amateur and semi professional leagues were formed but few survived.

In 1938, the first of what was hoped to be a regular 'Baseball Test Series' between England and the USA was organised. England was largely represented by Canadians who had been playing in the John Moores Professional League, and they won with ease. Although the promoters never claimed the series to be anything more than it was, the International Baseball Association later credited 'England's' hollow victory as deciding the first Amateur World Championship.

Clubs faced many problems in reorganising after the Second World War, but progress was steady for a decade in Liverpool, Manchester, Birmingham, Humberside and London. Unfortunately, there was then a series of squabbles within baseball, and between baseball and softball, which hampered baseball's development in Britain for many years. As recently as 1978 the London Association had less than ten teams but the resurgence of interest in recent seasons resulted in twenty-four teams playing in three eight-team divisions in 1985. This had increased to 33 teams in four divisions in 1987 organised by BBF (South), which played between May and August.

Scottish Amicable Assurance Society announced in April 1987 that it would be contributing £100,000 a year for three years to 'provide administrative support, publicity, coaching and umpiring clinics, sponsorship of the existing National Club Championship, and to set up and manage a new National League'.

Scottish Amicable's General Manager said that he was confident that the British Baseball Federation (formerly the BABSF), 'will use the sponsorship money effectively to nurture grass roots baseball through exciting development programmes and establish baseball as a leading summer sport in this country'.

The six teams taking part in the National League in 1987 – Southern Tigers, London Warriors, Nottingham Knights, Mersey Mariners, Lancashire Red Sox, and Humberside County Bears – played a round robin league between 6 June and 15 August, select players with clubs in each of amateur baseball's current strongholds. The national club Championship Final was on 20 September, and the Knockout Cup Final a week later.

BRITISH BASEBALL NATIONAL CUP FINALS

BASEBALL ASSOCIATION OF GREAT BRITAIN AND IRELAND

1890 Preston North End Amateurs beat Birmingham Amateurs 42–15, and 42–7

NATIONAL BASEBALL ASSOCIATION

1892 Middlesbrough 26–16 St Thomas's Derby
1893 Thespians London 33–6 St Augustine's Darlington
1894 Thespians London 38–14 Stockton-on-Tees
1895 Derby 20–16 Fuller's London
1896 Wallsend on Tyne 16–10 Remington's London
1897 Derby 30–7 Middlesbrough
1899 Derby 14–3 Nottingham Forest
1900 Nottingham Forest 17–16 Derby

BRITISH BASEBALL ASSOCIATION

1906 Tottenham Hotspur 16–5 Nondescripts
1907 Clapton Orient 8–7 Fulham
1908 Tottenham Hotspur 6–5 Leyton
1909 Clapton Orient 6–4 Leyton
1910 Brentford 20–5 West Ham
1911 Leyton 6–5 Crystal Palace

NATIONAL BASEBALL ASSOCIATION (2)

1934 Hatfield Liverpool 13–12 Albion Liverpool
1935 New London 7–1 Rochdale Greys
1936 White City London 9–5 Catford Saints
1937 Hull 5–1 Romford Wasps
1938 Rochdale Greys 1–0 Oldham Greyhounds
1939 Halifax 9–5 Rochdale Greys

BASEBALL ASSOCIATION LIMITED

1948 Liverpool Robins 13–0 Thames Board Mills Purfleet
1949 Hornsey Red Sox 10–5 Liverpool Cubs
1950 Burtonwood USAF Bees 23–2 Hornsey Red Sox
1951 Burtonwood USAF Bees 9–2 Ruislip USAF Rockets

BRITISH BASEBALL FEDERATION

1959 Thames Board Mills Purfleet 12–3 East Hull Aces
1960 Thames Board Mills Purfleet 6–1 Liverpool Tigers
1962 Liverpool Tigers 8–3 East Hull Aces
1963 East Hull Aces 8–6 Garrington's Bromsgrove

BRITISH BASEBALL ASSOCIATION (2)

1965 Kingston Aces Hull 4–2 Stretford Saints Manchester

NATIONAL BASEBALL LEAGUE (UK)

1966 Stretford Saints Manchester 3–1 Liverpool Aces
1967 Liverpool Mormon Yankees 4–2 Beckenham Blue Jays
1968 Hull Aces 4–1 Hull Royals
1969 Watford Sun-Rockets 8–7 Liverpool Trojans
1970 Hull Royals 3–1 Hull Aces
1971 Liverpool NALGO Tigers 8–3 Hull Aces
1972 Hull Aces beat Hull Royals (official score not known)

BRITISH AMATEUR BASEBALL FEDERATION

1973 Burtonwood Yanks 23–2 Hull Aces
1974 Nottingham Lions 5–3 Hull Royals
1975 Liverpool NALGO Tigers 5–3 Nottingham Lions
1976 Liverpool Trojans 5–4 Kensington Spirit of '76 London
1977 Golders Green Sox 9–5 Hull Aces

BRITISH AMATEUR BASEBALL AND SOFTBALL FEDERATION

1978 Liverpool Trojans 14–12 Crawley Giants
1979 Golders Green Sox 9–7 Hull Aces
1980 Liverpool Trojans 12–1 Hull Aces
1981 London Warriors 23–3 Hull Aces
1982 London Warriors 16–7 Liverpool Trojans
1983 Cobham Yankees London 10–3 Hull Mets
1984 Croydon Blue Jays 9–8 Hull Mets
1985 Hull Mets 10–8 London Warriors
1986 Cobham Yankees 12–0 Hull Mets

BRITISH BASEBALL FEDERATION (2)

1987

For information about baseball in Britain contact:
British Baseball Federation, 197 Newbridge Road, Hull, HU9 2LR.

For details about amateur baseball played around the world, contact:
International Baseball Association, Capital Centre, 251 N. Illinois Street, Suite 975, Indianapolis, Illinois 46204, USA.

MAJOR LEAGUE BASEBALL ALL-TIME HOME RUN HITTERS (start of 1987)

Total	Name	Batted	Career	Age at Retirement
755	Hank Aaron	r	1954–76	36
714	Babe Ruth	l	1914–35	40
660	Willie Mays	r	1951–73	42
586	Frank Robinson	r	1956–76	41
573	Harmon Killebrew	r	1954–75	39
548*	Reggie Jackson	l	1967–	now 41
536	Mickey Mantle	sw	1951–68	37
534	Jimmie Foxx	r	1925–45	37
521	Ted Williams	l	1939–60	41
521	Willie McCovey	l	1959–80	42
512	Eddie Mathews	l	1952–68	37
512	Ernie Banks	r	1953–71	40
511	Mel Ott	l	1926–47	38
495**	Mike Schmidt	r	1972–	now 37

*Reggie Jackson, now with the Oakland Athletics of the AL, passed 550, and Mike Schmidt, who plays for the Philadelphia Phillies of the NL, reached 500 during the third week of the 1987 regular season. Both events were in danger of being upstaged by celebrations to mark the retirement of Julius 'Dr J' Erving, the basketball star with the Philadelphia 76ers of the NBA.

**Mike Schmidt's 500th home run was hit in the ninth inning, with two men out and two runners on base, and gave Philadelphia a much needed 8–6 victory at Chicago's Wrigley Field.

MLB TERMS AND ABBREVIATIONS

Batting average: Divide the number of at bats into the number of hits.

Batting championship: A player must have over 502 plate appearances.

Earned run average: Multiply the number of earned runs by nine, then divide that total by the number of innings pitched.

ERA leader: To qualify, a pitcher must have pitched over 162 innings.

Games back (behind) G.B.: This most useful statistic shows the number of games each team is behind the division leader. It is calculated by adding together the difference in wins and the difference in losses between the two teams involved, then dividing that number by two.

Innings pitched: This number may have ⅓ or ⅔ after it. This fraction means that one or two batters were out.

Line scores: Scorecards for baseball games have been published in American newspapers for over 130 years. Where space allows they may be full box scores, but more usually they are the all-in-a-line score given in this book for the 1986 World Series (see page 116–18).

The visiting team always bats first, so it is listed above the home side. The runs scored in each inning (from the first to the ninth) are listed in sets of three numbers. There will be extra numbers if teams played extra innings because scores were tied after nine stanzas. An 'x' shows that the home team did not have to bat in the final inning as it had already won the game.

After the dash there is a set of three numbers showing the total runs, hits, and errors by each team. The winner is the club which has scored more runs.

Below these two lines, are, or come, the names of the starting pitcher followed by any relieving pitchers used (with the inning they came into the game given in brackets) and finally, the catcher's name with his club's name abbreviated. This is done for both teams with each divided by a semi-colon.

The winning and losing pitchers are listed with their season or playoff record, plus any relieving pitcher credited with a save.

Next, the total runners left on base, any home runs hit, any game-winning RBI and, finally, the time the game took and the attendance.

Magic number: This is how many more wins are needed to clinch the division. Take the number of games yet to be played in the regular season, add one, then subtract the number of games ahead in the loss column of the standings from the closest opponents.

Percentage: Divide the number of games won by the total games won and lost.

Rookie: In the majors, a rookie will not have a total of more than 130 or bats or 50 innings pitched, or been on the active roster of a club for more than 45 days during the 25-player limit.

Run batted in: An RBI is credited to a batter when a run is scored as a direct result of an 'offensive action' (e.g. a base hit, forced advance or an error), provided that less than two batters are out and the runner on third base could have scored despite the error.

GWRBI: The Game-Winning RBI is the run batted in that gives a team the lead it never relinquishes.

Abbreviations of playing positions: if = infielder, of = outfielder, 1b = first base, 2b = second base, 3b = third base, ss = shortstop, lf = left fielder, cf = centre fielder, rf = right fielder, c = catcher, p = pitcher, rp = relief pitcher, dh = designated hitter, sw = switch hitter, lh = left-handed, rh = right-handed.

Designated hitter: A player, designated at the start of a game to bat in place of the pitcher, without causing the pitcher to be removed from the game.

The designated hitter in the World Series

For the 1986 World Series there was a change to the designated hitter (DH) rule. Since 1976, the DH had been permitted in all World Series games in even numbered years, but not allowed at all in odd years. In 1986 the DH was allowed to be used by both teams in games played in the AL ballpark (Boston) but not in the NL stadium (New York Mets). Although the AL team has only won two of the five World Series in which the designated hitter had been allowed, Boston seemed to have been put at a disadvantage by not having designated hitter Don Baylor available in every game. This rule applies again in 1987.

All-Star Game Records 1933–86
Most appearances: 24 Stan Musial 1943–63
24 Willie Mays 1954–72
24 Hank Aaron 1955–75
Most times on winning team:
17 Willie Mays
17 Hank Aaron
Most times on losing team:
15 Brooks Robinson
Youngest player: 19yrs 7m 24 days Dwight Gooden 1984
Oldest player: 47yrs 7 days Leroy Paige 1953

MAJOR LEAGUE 1987 REGULAR SEASON STATISTICS GRID (to fill in)

AMERICAN LEAGUE

WEST	won	lost	Pct.	Games Behind
1.				
2.				
3.				
4.				
5.				
6.				
7.				

AMERICAN LEAGUE

EAST	won	lost	Pct.	Games Behind
1.				
2.				
3.				
4.				
5.				
6.				
7.				

Individual Leaders (AL regular season record since 1900 in brackets)

Batting: Average   (.422)
Hits   (257)
Runs   (177)
Runs batted in   (184)
Home runs   (61)
Stolen bases   (130)

Pitching:
Total victories   (41)
Strikeouts   (383)
Earned run average   (1.14)
Innings pitched   (464)
Saves   (46)

NATIONAL LEAGUE

WEST	won	lost	Pct.	Games Behind
1.				
2.				
3.				
4.				
5.				
6.				

NATIONAL LEAGUE

EAST	won	lost	Pct.	Games Behind
1.				
2.				
3.				
4.				
5.				
6.				

Individual Leaders (NL regular season record since 1900 in brackets)

Batting: Average   (.424)
Hits   (254)
Runs   (158)
Runs batted in   (190)
Home runs   (56)
Stolen bases   (118)

Pitching:
Total victories   (37)
Strikeouts   (382)
Earned run average   (1.12)
Innings pitched   (434)
Saves   (45)

1987 ALCS

Probable Fixture Dates	Venue	1987 ALCS		1	2	3	4	5	6	7	8	9	TOTALS Runs-Hits-Errors
Runs scored in each inning													
1. Tues 6 Oct	at West	E											
		W											
2. Wed 7 Oct	at West	E											
		W											
3. Fri 9 Oct	at East	W											
		E											
4. Sat 10 Oct	at East	W											
		E											
(5. if needed) Sun 11 Oct	at East	W											
		E											
(6. if needed) Tues 13 Oct	at West	E											
		W											
(7. if needed) Wed 14 Oct	at West	E											
		W											

Winner of 1987 American League Pennant: _____

1987 NLCS

Probable Fixture Dates	Venue	1987 NLCS		1	2	3	4	5	6	7	8	9	TOTALS Runs-Hits-Errors
Runs scored in each inning													
1. Tues 6 Oct	at East	W											
		E											
2. Wed 7 Oct	at East	W											
		E											
3. Fri 9 Oct	at West	E											
		W											
4. Sat 10 Oct	at West	E											
		W											
(5. if needed) Sun 11 Oct	at West	E											
		W											
(6. if needed) Tues 13 Oct	at East	W											
		E											
(7. if needed) Wed 14 Oct	at East	W											
		E											

Winner of 1987 National League Pennant: _____

Probable Fixture Dates	Venue	**1987 WORLD SERIES**	Runs scored in each inning									TOTALS
			1	2	3	4	5	6	7	8	9	Runs-Hits-Errors
1. Sat 17 Oct	at AL	NL										
		AL										
2. Sun 18 Oct	at AL	NL										
		AL										
3. Tues 20 Oct	at NL	AL										
		NL										
4. Wed 21 Oct	at NL	AL										
		NL										
(5. if needed) Thurs 22 Oct	at NL	AL										
		NL										
(6. if needed) Sat 24 Oct	at AL	NL										
		AL										
(7. if needed) Sun 25 Oct	at AL	NL										
		AL										

Winner of 1987 World Series:

MAJOR LEAGUE BASEBALL ON RADIO

This list of frequencies should help the ever increasing number of baseball fans in the UK who are staying up late during the summer to listen to Major League games broadcast by the Armed Forces Radio and Television Service, on AFN Europe.

AFRTS SHORTWAVE RADIO FREQUENCIES

Broadcasting to Europe since 29 July 1986 from transmitters at Greenville, N. Carolina, and Bethany, Ohio.

0100–0700 UTC. 6030 kHz 49m band
0900–1100 UTC. 9590 kHz 31m band
1100–2200 UTC. 15430 kHz 19m band

The AFRTS Broadcast Centre moved to Sun Valley, California, in November 1986. Due to ionospheric changes the reception tends to 'fade and return' every few minutes, is subject to interference from adjacent stations, and slips slightly across the dial during the evening. If reception gets too poor, AFRTS alters the frequencies after due warning.

AFN EUROPE RADIO FREQUENCIES
Medium Wave (AM):
 873 kHz Frankfurt
1107 kHz Munich and 3 other towns,
1143 kHz Kaiserslautern and 17 others
1485 kHz Garmisch and 7 others

VHF (FM):
In West Germany between
87.9 MHz Berlin and 104.6 Heidelberg.

In the Netherlands between
89.2 MHz Schinnen and 98.0 New Amsterdam.

In Belgium between
101.5 MHz SHAPE and 106.2 Kleine Brogel.